GOVERNANCE OF INDIA

DEDICATION

Dedicated to the everlasting memory of my revered parents, Dhurendhar Singh (L) and teacher Shri Jai Mangal Sinha, who have been a perennial source of inspiration and encouragement to me.

About the Author

R.N. Prasad is Professor of Public Administration and Head, Department of Public Administration, North-Eastern Hill University, Mizoram Campus, Aizawal. He has been teaching Political Science and Public Administration for well over three decades.

He has participated in several local, regional, national and international seminars, conferences, workshops and contributed numerous research papers.

He has more than seventy published research articles and book reviews in both the edited volumes and academic/professional journals of national and international repute to his credit.

He has written/edited a number of books on regional studies including *Government and Politics in Mizoram*; *Political and Economic Development of Mizoram*; *Autonomy movements in Mizoram*; *Landmarks: A Study of Public Administration in Mizoram* and *Public Administration in North-East India*.

He is an Honorary Secretary of the Indian Institute of Public Administration, Mizoram Regional Branch, Aizawal and editor of its Annula Journal—*Administrative Review*.

GOVERNANCE OF INDIA

Issues and Perspectives

R.N. Prasad
Professor and Head,
Department of Public Administration,
North-Eastern Hill University,
Mizoram Campus, Aizawal

CONCEPT PUBLISHING COMPANY, NEW DELHI - 110059

ISBN 81-7022-974-X

First Published 2002

Published and Printed by
Ashok Kumar Mittal
Concept Publishing Company
A/15-16, Commercial Block, Mohan Garden,
NEW DELHI -110059 (India)

Phones : 5351460, 5351794
Fax : 091-11-5357103
E-mail : *publishing@conceptpub.com*

PREFACE

The Governance of India has two major land marks : constitutionalism and planned economic development. Regarding constitutional objectives, the Constitution of India provides for sovereign, socialist, secular and democratic republic of India. The liberal democratic Constitution of India has its major endeavour to secure for the citizens of the country social, political and economic justice, liberty; equality; dignity of individuals and unity and integrity of nation. These constitutional objectives have been enshrined in the preamble and the chapters 3 and 4 (Fundamental Rights and Directive Principles of State Policy) of the Constitution. With a view to achieving these goals/objectives, the governance of the country has adopted the planned economic development. Besides, other chapters of the Constitution also provide for the administrative machinery and mechanism to facilitate implementation/translation of the constitutional humane objectives/goals into practice and reality in order to uplift the socio-economic conditions of the people and to provide for them new opportunities to lead a meaningful and dignified life. Briefly, the basic objective of governance in India needs to be based on the principles enshrined in the Constitution and institutions which are linked with democratic process in a significant manner. In other words, the inter-related and inter-connected institutional arrangements for governance are democratic participation, decentralisation of powers on the basis of federalism (national, regional, sub-regional and local levels) state led multiple programmes for economic regeneration and political regime; which does not show any preferences on the basis of discrimination of any sort in a pluralistic society of India.

An attempt has been made to revitalise public administration to translate the constitutional objectives into practice for the greatest good of the greatest number at various levels and stages through recommendations of various Committees/Commissions on administrative reforms and its allied areas; Constitution of several statutory and non-statutory bodies at different levels—like Committees of Legislatures, Vigilance Commission, Planning Commission, proposed ombudsmen, PRIs etc. and special efforts like positive intervention of judiciary (P.I.L.), establishment of consumer fora, rolling back of government and its substitution by voluntary and co-operative bodies, attempts at mobilising public opinion as a direct and indirect action. However, despite all these efforts, liberal democratic governance of India has failed to make a significant impact on public psyche due to its slide down the slope as is evident in different spheres since Independence. It is widely felt that the pace has gathered alarming momentum in view of many unhealthy developments in politics; which deeply affect other segments of society. Now nothing seems to arrest the institutional deterioration and decline of values in general.

Even after more than 50 years of experience and experimentation, there has been big gap between the policy formulation and its implementation, as regards various aspects and issues in administration. As the fact remains true, the Indian governance has been strong on assurances and weak on performance. Therefore, the results have not been commensurate with the growing needs and aspirations of the Indian masses especially the poor/down trodden /*dalits*. Jawaharlal Nehru, the first Prime Minister has correctly expressed his desappointment particularly in his last years that he could not bring about the desired improvements in our administrative system, its organisation, structure, relationships, and its working. However, besides persistence of problems and challenges of the governance of India with incresing severity, it has been also witnessed in succeeding decades exceleration in the process of degeneration in the country's socio-political and administrative scenario. The dissatisfaction with the existing level of governance, the adoption of New-Economic Policy of Liberalisation, Privatisation and Globalisation and western model of development administration along capitalist lines, a large number of social, political and economic challenges and crises have emerged. Poverty and unemployment are on the rise. The disparities between the rich and the poor owing to the capitalist model of modernisation have been increasing. The benefits of the economic growth have not yet reached the millions of the poor and neglected Indian masses, though the economic growth has been achieved. The New Economic Policy has not produced genuine economic growth with equity and social justice and Structural-Adjustment Programme (SAP) has attacked the conditions of life and work of the working people and poor, marginalising women in various aspects of their existence. In reality, the market led development and governance based on capitalist lines are contrary to the preamble provisions of the Constitution of India. The fact is that the class elites in politics and bureaucracy have facilitated the development of capitalist class in India with full support of the Indian state. It is, thus, obvious that the capitalist class and the government are working in close harmony and co-operation with one another. Briefly, the state is the promoter of capitalism, because the capitalists are controlling the state through muliple linkages and alliances.

The situation has become so alarming now that even the law and order situation in many parts of the country, rural as well as urban, presents a depressing picture. With burgeoning crime, people complain that they have no security of peaceful living despite a large number of police and security forces maintained by both the Central and the State governments. There are other burning issues also like propriety in the exercise of administrative discretion; paralysis of political will and capacity for decision-making; insurgency on the borders and terrorist activities within the country; various kinds of mafia and musclemen running a parallel administration and the unwillingness or inability of crime prevention and punitive authorities of the state to coutain them, mounting administrative corruption and political venality, leading to an erosion in the credibility and effectiveness of democratic governing institutions. People expect a prompt and effective response to their problems and concerns. There seems to be in society, especially among youth increasing indifference, apathy, nihilism, despondency, negativism and a lack of trust as regards the capability or the desire of the present politico-administrative governance to act purposefully, fairly and impartially. This does not bode well for future governance of India.

Governance, however, is not a finished product. It is a dynamic concept. In simple terms, governance can be considered the citizen friendly, citizen caring and responsive administration. The concept of humane governance puts people at the centre of all governance policies, strategies and actions. The basic precepts of the human development model are to improve the capabilities and expand the opportunities of all people irrespective of class, caste, gender and ethnicity. The concept of humane governance takes this model forward by asserting that governance, if it is to promote human development, has to be not just pro-peole, or people centred, it has to be owned by the people. It encompasses fast changing social, political and economic, milieu along with international environment and conditions of operational governance. There is need to remodel the concept and institutions of governance. Therefore, a major structural shift and institutional change in the existing socio-economic model on capitalist lines, exploitative social and property relations and the pursuit of the new economic policy or market economy framework have to be considered/made. The positive role of the state in resolving social, political and economic conflicts seriously affecting the Indian masses living below the poverty line is needed/emphasised. The Indian state/political system; in a nutshell, needs to be redesigned to respond the problems/challenges confronting the Indian governance, which are arising out of the failures of the state and nation-building. To bring about changes in the good governance has to be a continuing exercise. It is in this background that the book under publication dealing with the confronting problems/ issues of the Indian governance since Independence and their possible resolution, will be helpful both for academic and practical purposes of humane governance.

The book contains fourteen chapters on various problems/issues and perspectives like social, politico-administrative, and economic of the Indian governance. These chapters have already been published in academic and professional journals of national and international repute which are reproduced in this volume. Acknowledgements are due to the professional and academic journals. The paper on "Socio-Political Development in India during the Last Fifty Years" by Dr. H.Thansanga has been presented at the seminar on "Fifty Years of India's Independence" organised by the Government of Mizoram in March, 2000. Shri P. Chakraborty's paper on "Judicial Activism, Legislature and the Common Man" has already been published in the Mizoram Legislative Assembly Silver Jubilee Souvenir, 1997. They have given their papers and also consented to get the papers published in this volume. Dr. H. Thansanga, Education Minister, Mizoram (Ex), is the Chairman of the Indian Institute of Public Administration, Mizoram Regional Branch. Shri P. Chakraborty is Secretary to the Government of Mizoram I/c Law and Judicial Departments. I am extremely thankful to them for contributing the papers to this volume.

I express my profound sense of gratefulness and sincere respect to Prof. Arvind K.Sharma, Vice-Chancellor, Mizoram University, Aizawal for his sincere guidance, motivation, inspiration, workable academic suggestion and unstinted help in building up of my academic career consistently.

Prof. A.K. Agarwal, Department of Economics, Mizoram University, Aizawal deserves my thanks for his unstinted academic suggestions and guidance.

My thanks are due to Dr. C. Lalkima, esteemed colleague in the Department for his academic support and cooperation in all matters.

For sharing many odd responsibilities of this volume's proofs correction and other works of academic nature, I accord thanks in my heart to my former student, present colleague and research scholar Lalneihzovi.

I cannot express adequately in words the profound gratitude and heartfult thanks, I owe to my wife Mrs. Shanti Prasad for the inconvenience she had to undergo due to my preoccupation with this modest study.

I feel pleasure in conveying my thanks to Shri Ashok Kumar Mittal, Concept Publishing Company, New Delhi-59 for publishing this volume promptly and expeditiously to the entire satisfaction of the clientele.

R.N. PRASAD

CONTENTS

Preface 5

1. Emerging Challenges of the Governance of India 13
2. Conflicts arising out of Contradictions in Indian Political System : Their Implications for Internal Security 43
3. Prospects of Coalition Government in India 63
4. Secularism in India : Problems and Perspectives 78
5. New Panchayati Raj System and People's Aspirations 92
6. Our Goals for Twenty-First Century : (a) Economic, (b) Social and (c) Administrative : Some Suggestions 99
7. Women's Participation in Politics and Decision-Making : Problems and Prospects 110
8. National Agenda of the New Government : Administrative Dimensions—An Appraisal 124
9. India's Population Policy : Challenges Ahead and Strategies Therefor 134
10. Conflicts of Plural Society and their Impact on Internal Security 141
11. University and Political Development in Independent India 164
12. Socio-Political Development in India during the Last Fifty Years 174
13. Judicial Activism, Legislature and the Common Man 190
14. Review of the Indian Constitution 207

Bibliography 219

Index 222

1

EMERGING CHALLENGES OF THE GOVERNANCE OF INDIA

The governance of post-Independent India has two major landmarks : constitutionalism and planned economic transformation/ development leading to the growth of private corporate sector/ capitalist development. As regards the constitutional objectives, the Constitution of India provides for sovereign, democratic socialist and secular republic of India. The liberal democratic constitution of India has its major endeavour to secure for citizens of the country social; political and economic justice; liberty; equality; dignity of individuals; and unity and integrity of the nation. These constitutional objectives have been enshrined in chapters III and IV (Fundamental Rights and Directive Principles of State Policy) of the Constitution. To achieve these goals/objectives, the country has adopted a planned economic development to uplift the socio-economic conditions of the people and to provide for them new opportunities to lead a meaningful and dignified life. The country's approach to modernisation/development does not only mean to augment the resources but to build institutional framework to the fulfilment of the growing needs and aspirations of the people. To set up political and administrative machineries/institutions as a basic requirements for the successful implementation of the plan was emphasised. The basic requirements thus include an agreement based on active co-operation of the people, and an efficient administrative set-up having personnel of requisite capacity and quality. In another words, the inter-related and inter-connected institutional arrangements for governance are democratic participation, decentralisation of powers on the basis of federalism, state-led multiple programmes for economic, regeneration and a political regime which does not show any preferences on the basis of discrimination of any sort in a pluralistic society of India. An effort needs to deepen the quality of democratic participation in governance at national, regional, sub-regional and local levels in the country. Briefly, the basic objective of governance in India needs to be based on the principles enshrined in the Constitution and institutions which are linked with democratic process in a significant manner.

Apart from, a pertinent question is : how has the liberal democratic state of India facilitated the growth of private corporate sector/capitalism through Five Year plans? In the last thirty five years through Sixth Five Year plans, the government has invested about Rs. 25,000 crore in the development of steel, heavy machine, tool, transport, power and other essential infrastructural activities. This critical role of the state has facilitated the growth of private corporate sector in India. This is not the only activity which the government had undertaken to develop capitalism. The capitalist class needed resources for investment and this required mobilisation of domestic savings in the country. By nationalising the life insurance business in 1956 and private banks in 1969, the government controlled mobilizable savings and assisted the capitalist class to diversify their investments and products. All major private investors/Big Business Houses in the country are today supported by the public financial institutions in their industrial activities.

A pertinent question arises : why has the private corporate sector developed so enormously when the state is the chief controller and regulator of the economy? Why is the state handing over the resources mobilized by the nationalised life insurance business and commercial banks to the private investors for building private industrial empires? The prosperity and development of the private Big Houses and the emergence of the monopoly houses with full support of the state deserve serious explanation. It is thus obvious that the capitalist class and the government are working in close harmony and co-operation with onc another.

Thus, the development of capitalist class in India should not be viewed in isolation but in an integrated manner with its class allies in politics and bureaucracy. This alliance explains the smooth development of Indian capitalism with full support of the Indian state. Briefly, capitalism is developing in India in a conscious manner and the state is its promotor because capitalists are controlling the state through multiple linkage and alliances.[1]

Meaning of Governance

The term 'governance' has wider meaning than that of the term 'Government' Government refers to the machinery and institutional arrangements of exercising the sovereign power for serving the internal and external interests of the political community, whereas governance means the process as well as, the result of making authoritative decisions for the benefit of the society.[2] Governance also refers to the forms of political system and the manner in which power is exercised in utilizing the country's economic and social resources for development.[3] It deals with the capacity of the government to design, formulate and implement policies, and in general, to discharge government's functions. Governance is associated with efficient and effective administration in a democratic framework.[4] It is equivalent to purposive and development oriented administration which is committed to improvement of quality of life of the mass people. It implies the high level of organisational effectiveness. It also relates to the capacity of the centre of power of political and administrative system to cope up with the emerging challenges of the society. It refers to the adoption of new values of governance with a view to establish greater efficiency, legitimacy and credibility of the system. In simple terms, governance can be considered the citizen friendly, citizen caring and responsive administration.[5]

It may be further added that to the 1999. Human Development Report on South-Asia written by late Mahbub-ul-Haq, the concept of humane governance puts people at the centre of all governance policies, strategies and actions. The basic precepts of the human development model are to improve the capabilities and expand the opportunities of all people irrespective of class, caste, gender and ethnicity. The concept of humane governance takes this model forward by asserting that governance, if it is to promote human development, has to be not just pro-people, or people centred, it has to be owned by people.[6] The Report further says that humane governance is governance, indeed good governance, which is dedicated to securing human development. It requires effective participation of people in state, civil society, and private sector activities that are conducive to human development. It further enjoins the state, civil society and private sector to help build capacities which will meet the basic needs of all people, particularly women, children and the poor. Humane governance will also ensure that human development is sustainable.[7] Briefly, to the Report, humane governance has three inter-linked dimensions : economic, political and civic. Economic governance consists of those factors required to sustain economic development. Political governance is defined as the use of institutions by the government to govern, and civic governance as the right and responsibility of the governed to participate in and promote good governance.[8] It is to be expected that a country with high economic, political and civic governance would also have high human development. Humane governance can only be achieved by combining all the three dimensions of economic, political and civic governance. One dimension does not come before another. They must occur in unison for the meaning/ concept of humane governance to be realised. The Report further says that an effective way to nurture a pro-people political system is to guard against the personalisation and concentration of power. This involves separating power among state institutions–the parliament, the executives and judiciary to serve as checks and balances. For any process, to work, the rules must be observed transparently, neutrally, and universally. Institutions that are strong, provide the necessary resilience to the political system/process by enshrining the rule of law.[9] Besides, R. Venkataraman, Ex-President of India has also identified some of the ingredients of good government. To him, a government is stable and truly representative of the majority of people, maintains its territiorial integrity and national sovereignty, accelerates economic growth and development, ensures the welfare of all sections of people and renders justice without delay.[10]

The main objectives of governance concern the basic goals of the society as incorporated in the Constitution, public policies and plan documents. Besides the set-up of institutions and framework to maintain law and order, the state is needed to frame rules and regulations by which politico-administrative system governs itself. The state in some societies, plays a very significant role to create/establish basic infrastructure for economic development and provision of such services which may lead to social justice. The degree of involvement of politico-administrative system may vary from society to society. Since Independence, there has been an attempt to achieve these aspects of governance.

Governance Performance

Since post-Independence period, there has been a significant endeavour to bring about structural changes in the administrative set-up to fulfil the growing needs and aspirations of the people as enshrined in the Constitution and various plan documents. Many public sector enterprises, were set up to bring about rapid industrial development. At the end of 15 years, India had become one of the top fifteen countries in the world in industrial production. The liberal democratic state of India has endeavoured to develop rural areas through decentralisation and participation of the rural people. The governance of India has also aimed at bringing, though, in a phased manner a new technology and modern techniques of management to bring about a sound system of governance.

Although the liberal democratic political system of India has adopted the capitalist path of development and constitutionalism suiting to capitalist oriented society, yet the political system since independence has achieved a considerable success/progress in some fields/cases. Political and administrative continuity with an independent justiciary, free press, federalism and secularism despite the size and multi-cultural aspects of the Indian society has been maintained/sustained. In other words, the country's single achievement has been the preservation and reinforcement of liberal democracy, the foundation of which are laid by the Constitution seeking to ensure an extensive set of rights to the citizenry. The promise in the Constitution's Preamble, of securing for all Indian masses "liberty of thought, expression, belief, faith and worship" has been by and large translated into reality, warding off in the process manifold assaults from vested interests still wielding considerable influence over the Indian society, the post colonial state of India has recorded a considerable industrial growth and attained a diversified industrial base and has capabilities in basic areas of science and technology. The country has the world's third largest-cadre/pool of active scientific and technical manpower, more than 4 millions. The country has also joined nuclear club with its 1974 and 1998 Pokhran nuclear tests and thereby achieved a place of prominence among the developed and developing countries. The country's performance in quadrupling food production at the macro level in the last four and a half decades deserves commendation.

Briefly, the country is the world's fifth biggest national product in terms of sheer value of output. The state has somewhat transformed the colonial administration to the one which is responding to the need of people to an extent. The liberal democratic state of India has, since July 1991, has brought about changes in the annal of economic administration by adopting New Economic Policy of Liberalisation, privatisation and globalisation which contradicts the Preamble provisions.

Challenges

India has evolved a unique state system which is based on democratic participation, federal arrangements of governance and secular and socially accommodation process of modernisation. Every pillar of this system is in deep crisis and the state functionaries are making fundamental compromises on every basic social goal of the state. A system collapses when the state functionaries do not struggle to uphold the basic values or when they fail to apply appropriate correctives to restructure the state. The USSR and Yugoslavia have been obliterated from the world map because the leaders of these countries failed to rectify serious distortions of their systems. Similarly in India, many fundamental steps have to be taken to face the emerging multi-dimensional challenges if the country wants to move forward on the basis of democratic, federal and secular system.

Inspite of all the transformations/changes, the Indian common masses at large are not satisfied with the performance of governance (politico-administrative system). Democratic legitimacy of the state is strengthened on the basis of its performance and if the citizens accept that their rulers are genuinely accountable to them. But the Indian state has a low level of legitimacy among the common people. The socio-economic problems/grievances of the people are increasing and they think of the administrative system to be inefficient, irresponsive and corrupt. Accountability in the delivery of public services has been shockingly poor public resources have not been utilized effectively. Poverty and unemployment are on the rise. Poverty anywhere is a threat to prosperity everywhere. The entire politico-administrative system is non-transparent. There is no perceptible change in bringing about economic development, social justice and restructure in the existing governance or the existing socio-politico economic power structure. The credibility of the public institutions is declining and the people are losing faith in the politico-administrative system. Besides, the dissatisfaction with the existing level of governance and western model of development administration along capitalist lines, a large number of social, political and economic challenges and crises have emerged. Owing to political and social mobilisation, the needs and aspirations of the people have increased. Apart from the disparities between the rich and the poor owing to the capitalist model of modernization have been increasing. The benefits of economic growth have not yet reached the millions of the poor/neglected Indian masses, though the economic growth has been achieved. But social justice and equity have not been established because political power has been exercised by the rural urban rich and the industrial and commercial classes for their benefits and advancements. Gradually, the institution of private property is being strengthened in India.

In other words, the distortions of the Indian political system as well as the non-translation of the Constitutional goals and socio-politico economic justice and as also equality of status and opportunity provisions into practice for the socio-economic development of the wretched conditions of the underprivileged and deprived/peripharised sections of the Indian society have given rise to social and political tensions/movements, insurgency, ethnic upsurge and agrarian social conflicts and the problems of law and order. Both the economic pressure of the international financial institutions and a weak domestic economic system have warranted a changed role of the administrative system. The people's participation through the new Panchayati Raj System has not taken off effectively or materialised so far, though, the democratic dacentralisation has long been regarded as a necessary condition of social, political and economic development. In brief, the capitalist path has succeeded in modernising the economy, but it has also led to deeping of crisis in the democratic governance.

Social Dimensions

Social justice means that all individuals have equal claims and equal opportunities to develop their individualities/ personalities and the disabilities attached to caste, sex, race, colour, creed, religion or nationality are removed. No doubt, the intelligence, aptitude and skill of the individuals varies and differs, but that does not mean that there should be discrimination in favour of a section of society to the detriment of others. In order to break the vicious caste culture and provide social justice to all, the Constitution of India has incorporated certain provisions in the chapters on Fundamental Rights and the Directive Principles of State Policy. But the liberal democratic state of India even after fifty years of Independence, has not yet translated these constitutional social justice provisions into practice owing to India being a capitalist oriented, class divided caste ridden and multi-religious society. Division of society into different classes being a feature of the capitalist society is a barrier to social justice.

Quality and coverage of family welfare has not been enhanced as expected. Education is both means as well as end result of development. It is also the most powerful instrument for the empowerment of the people. But education system in India is in a very bad shape. India has the highest rate of illiteracy in the world. The highest incidence of illiteracy is still among the weaker/deprived sections of society. Women and the girls have the least educational opportunities in India. There is little evidence of the equalization of the educational opportunity in our grossly unequal society. The poor and children suffer from malnutrition/diseases. More than half of the Indian population has no access to drinking water. There are great regional social inequalities, violence in society particularly against women, children and the underprivileged, and development induced displacement and ecological and environmental devastation. Child labour continues which is a result of poverty and unemployment. Poverty and unemployment questions are power questions rooted in the development model that the country has adopted, and the socio-economic power structure that obtains in the country. Both have been increasing since the adoption of the New Economic Policy of the government. Western development model and new package of policies have a jobless growth and cannot alleviate poverty. Food security to all poor people, all the time cannot be ensured without ensuring full and adequate security to earn livelihoods in the normal course of their activities. Nearly three-fourth of the population consume less than the needed calories. Record increments in the food prices for those below the poverty line add to the miseries of the poor causing wide spread distress. Public health has become a major casualty in the era of privatisation, liberalisation and globalisation. Child care is another area of major concern. Women's empowerment remains uneffective. Gender justice remains a distant goal. A similar problem exists in respect of socially and economically backward group like scheduled castes, scheduled tribes and other backward classes. Despite the policy of reservation, their socio-economic status has not improved. Even the policy has not been effectively implemented by the government. President K.R. Narayanan has, in this regard, significantly stated that India's privileged classes are spear heading a "counter-revolution against the affirmative action provided by Constitutional provisions".[11] Even the facilities extended to the weaker and disadvantaged sections of society have been cornered by a few influential rich families. Development and rehabilitative needs of persons with disabilities and other groups such as aged, street children, destitutes and the delinquent has not been achieved as expected. Provision of shelter to the slum dwellers and the rural poor has not yet been made. No effective land reforms have been undertaken to empower the rural weaker sections and women educationally and economically. Thus, there has been a rather dismal performance of the government in the social welfare sectors. It may be further added that the present government betrays no real concern for social issues. There is no vision, no planned and sustained effort to provide minimum social services to the deprived people in the foreseeable future. As the president has gently hinted, there seems to be a vested interest in keeping the large masses of the people illiterate and marginalized. Since the Narasimha Rao government, there has been no major increase in the Budget allocation for anti-poverty programmes.[12] While Amartya Sen has suggested that if India can spend more resources on education, health and implement land reforms, democratic strength of India can be restored.[13]

Political Crisis

Politics in every society is reflective of social situation and it is determined by social forces. This is one aspect of politics. The other aspect of politics is that it consciously intervenes in the social processes to contain negative forces and to initiate and encourage positive forces. In this conflict between the negative and positive forces, politics may assume a passive role or it may fight against the negative social forces. In any situation, politics cannot be inactive and on its response depends the directions of political development of a society. Further in a society which is involved in the process of grand transition, politics is expected to initiate the positive programmes of development and fight against forces which obstruct and hinder positive transitions. Politics of every developing country has to be purposive, and goal oriented and not merely manipulative. The purposive politics in a transitional society has to show a long term perspective because problems of transition cannot be initiated or managed in an adhoc and short term manner. To sum up, politics in a transitional society is influenced by the external and the internal factors and both are organically linked. If politics is positive and goal oriented, the external threats can be faced. If domestic politics is manipulative, short sighted, adhoc and crisis ridden, imperialism cannot be confronted.[14]

The above description provides a framework for analysis of the Indian political development of the last fifty years. If the Indian political development has to be seen in a dialectical manner, the positive and the negative factors have to be analysed in proper perspective. The democratic provisions such as democratic participation, federal arrangements of governance, secular and socially accommodation of modernisation, independent judiciary and public services are already enshrined in the Indian Constitution which need their translation into practice to be analysed. The most important achievement of the Indian political system is the politicisation of the Indian society during the last 50 years and, it has been further strengthened by people's participation through universal adult franchise and periodical elections to the Lok Sabha and the State Assemblies. The Universal adult franchise has gradually created high level of awareness among the voters including women and the poor people.

Another major political development of the last fifty years has been party alteration and peaceful transition from a defeated party to an electorally successful groups of a party or minority.

Coalition or minority politics owing to the plurality of the Indian society and regional diversities resulting into multiparty system has come to stay in the political governance of India. As a result, smaller parties and regional parties are having a significant role in governance and policy formulation but it is more related to political exigency resulting into a process of adopting and accommodation in policies formulation. Ideologically divergent allies/partners are bringing greater conflicts in governance.

In a multi-religious and multi-lingual country, by and large, secular politics has been able to harmonize different contending community and language group interests.

The 73rd Constitutional Amendment Act, 1992 relating to the Panchayati Raj Institutions gives political and financial powers to the grassroot level ensuring to protect the interest of the rural weaker sections. But to make it meaningful, socio-politico-economic power structure and property relations, generating disparities in the society have to be radically restructured, otherwise the weaker/ deprived section will not only be deprived to the development programmes but in most of the cases, they will be kept out of development process.

As the fact remains true, the liberal democratic state of India has facilitated the development of private capitalism by regulatory supportive and subsidy mechanisms since Independence. The expansion and diversification of private capitalism have taken place under the protective umbrella provided by the Indian government.[15]

The growing deep crisis of the Indian liberal democratic system is the result of many negative factors as they have emerged during the last fifty years:

1. The Indian political system has failed to implement the preamble provisions especially justice-social, political and economic as well as Directive Principles of State Policy of the Constitution. Articles (from 38 onwards) are the fundamentals for the socio-economic uplift of the people. These non-judicial principles need legal resonance to be accorded by the state.
2. Politics in India has become an instrument to exercise power and use public resources for class, group and personal benefits/ advancement. The road to political legitimacy is through ballot and electoral alliances based on caste and community. After winning the elections, the capitalist classes, landlords, and rich peasants and political-bureaucratic decision makers use their political power or political linkages for cornering public resources for their perpetual benefits/gains. The politics of purpose, goals and ideology has been replaced by politics of manipulation and cornering of public resources for personal benefits.
3. The Indian state has a low level of legitimacy among the people Because, the election process in India has eroded the democratic foundations of the state owing to the ugly role of money power, muscle power, caste/religion and open involvement of criminals in rigging the elections. Thus, the emerging distortions in the process of elections have weakened

the moral foundations of parliament and the state legislatures. The accountability of the elected representatives has always been weak because of the big social distance between the elected and voters. The democratic process has created a linkage based on social and economic networks and the mass of voters have no direct relationship with their elected representatives.

4. The poor citizens in India are mere voters, while the real beneficiaries of the state policies are the various power groups in society. This has created a serious negative situation. The neglected/deprived citizens have become alienated and some of them have taken to violence, socially and economically backward and exploited/frustrated groups are aggressive and violent. Poor or low or biased performance of the state has definitely weakened the democratic legitimacy of the state. Gunnar Myrdal in his seminal contribution the *Asian Drama* had characterized India as a "soft" state because of its incapacity to restructure social relations in the face of opposition of the powerful social groups. Our analysis is that India is "vulnerable" state because a large section of society feels that it has been marginalized by policies of neglect by the state.[16]

5. A democratic state gains strength if it can enforce its legality or rule of law in fair and impartial manner. Such a situation does not exist in India. The state functionaries break/bend normal laws and rules to accommodate the interests and pressures of the powerful groups. The citizens view the state functionaries as violators of law. This distortion has made the state incapable to implement the Constitutional provisions as well as to deal with serious situations of terrorism/insurgency and social movements/ethnic upsurge. If the state functionaries cannot be trusted as honest custodian of normal laws, it becomes impossible for the most people to support the Indian governance. *Mahabharata*, the great Indian epic of state craft said "Governance is treated in truth, and the people are rooted in the governance."

6. A democratic governance cannot function without an organized party system which in the country is in the process of disintegration. Political parties are confronted with a situation of shifting and transitory alliance. Many pure caste, ethnic and class parties of the property owners are emerging to challenge the Congress coalition. Competition to control political power is confined primarily to various components of the Congress coalition. Sectional interests are projected by many political parties and competition for sectional interests has accelerated social cleavages. People are losing faith in their leaders, rank and file of the political functionaries.
7. The Indian governance is in a serious crisis due to the distortions of federalism. The centralized federal system has generated the sentiments of alienation among many social and cultural groups. The state leaders have failed to realize the new social assertions of multiple groups which want a real share in power. Briefly, many social and cultural groups want to play a greater role within the democratic and federal state of India. The present centralised federation may be changed into co-operative and federal polity.
8. The democratic and federal structures of the state are under strain because secularism is under attack by competitive communalism of all major communities. A multi religious country cannot have a democratic and federal state without real secularism. Secularism cannot be possible, if secular politicians and bureaucrates are not managing it. It is only democracy based on secularism which will keep India united and the other road will lead to violence and disintegration of the country. To achieve this, the existing social structures and class character of the state power in India need to be restructured/reordered.
9. Caste and religion have become a powerful divisive forces in politics because all major democratic parties and leading social classes have fought their political battle of legitimacy on caste and religious basis. Secular politics in India was always weak and now its foundations are being challenged. The prospects of democratic and secular Indian political system are in doubt

because of the new strength shown by caste and religion in politics, and the incapability of democratic parties to fight against these divisive and disintegrating forces in politics.

10. Social violence in the rural and urban areas is increasing because the crisis of capitalist development is felt by the vulnerable and deprived strata of the society. The Indian political system is not able to protect the life of the poor because the state apparatus is controlled by the representatives of the exploiting classes. The private armies of landlords, the lumpen youth of the democratic parties, the communal and caste groups financed by smugglers are always able to inflict heavy physical injuries on the poor in rural and urban areas and state functionaries find themselves helpless to intervene because they cannot act against their financiers and political mentors.[17]
11. The feature of the political culture of the ruling class is the politicisation of the crime and the criminalisation of politics. Politicisation of crime involves the competitive use of anti-social force of the mobilisation of the party funds, for management of elections, for organising meeting and conferences and even for recruiting workers at lower levels from among anti-social elements. It also means the misuse of criminal intelligence as a political tool for black mailing political opponents. Criminalisation of politics means direct entry of criminals into the political parties and legislatures including parliament. It also means the use of criminal methods and tactics to influence political processes and procedures. The law-breakers are thus becoming the law-makers. To the Election Commission, in Uttar Pradesh Assembly alone out of 425 MLAs, 123 have criminal records. These are serious challenges to the Indian governance. It is unfortunate that no counter-vailing force to check criminalisation of politics is emerging.
12. De-culturation of politics is another challenge to the governance of India. Political culture of the ruling class has deflected from the past beliefs. Political culture of the ruling class is devoid of the norms of the decency. On the contrary, the despicable manoeuvres of the politicians abound. The ruling class "Obey no disciplines, no rule, no principle of public morality, display

no sense of public awareness and show no concern for the public weal"; and corruption is "even regarded as the hallmark of our leadership" and the ruling class is "drifting away from the people's and falling prey to "feudal oligarchy of power-broker' and influence peddlers".[18]

13. Unprincipled alliances, distortion of the Constitution to suit the powers that be destabilisation of institutional structures, loss of consensual paradigm of action, the pedestrian style of functioning, the crudities of private ambition and particularistic interests have hampered political development. The black money is on the rise, and speed money alone is a kind of grease to move smoothly the wheels of politico-bureaucratic decision makers. Besides, the political culture of the ruling class has either politicised bureaucracy or demoralised them to such an extent that bureaucracy is no longer a potential modernising agent. Most bureaucrats are at the back and call of the ruling class. Able and honest bureaucrates are either shunted out or sidelined. As a general rule, the bureaucracy has a fallen into decline.
14. Crippled political development is also a major concern. Because the political culture of the ruling class is hardly conducive to political development. It is drifting away from democratic norms and institutions. It is full of rancour of deep and long-lasting feelings of bitterness. Whatever, the ruling class is doing in the form of plannings, is designed to benefit the ruling class, the capitalist classes and the rich peasants; they are unable to bring the total transformation in the social structure of the society or the modes of production and the relations of production. As such, political structures have been clogged; it lacks meaning and predictability; and political activities falter to fulfil the desired objects and beliefs; the agencies of political socialisation have become weak. The national exchequer is being frittered away for party gains; the ruling class is jittery and is in panic and the instruments of political change have lost all vitality. The ruling class is torn with anxiety. The net result is that political development is frail and fragmented; it has been crippled seriously.[19]

15. The Indian political system is facing challenges from social groups and classes which are anti-democratic, anti-secular and anti-unity and diversity of federal system. Various segments of property owners are fighting their own better for supremacy over the political system. It has been seen in history that the exploiting classes compete against one another in politics when threat of revolutionary change is not present. This is the historical situation in India. Various segments of the exploiting classes are involved in political competition in which a segment of the exploiting class is able to corner maximum public resources. The capitalist classes, the rich peasants and the politico-bureaucratic decision makers are major competitors in politics, and while competing against one another, they also collaborate because, they are interested in the present political system which is giving dividends. The big business houses, the medium level capitalists, the landlords and rich peasants, the politico-bureaucratic decision-makers have all enhanced their assets and capacity to manipulate public resources through the existing political system and the victims of real crisis can be managed by brutalities of the state apparatus. The lumpen youth and the communal and caste warfare. Democratic legitimacy insulates ruling classes from public accountability and 48% of the population living below the poverty line can be subjected to tyranny of the landlords, and the high caste and communal mafias.[20]

Economic Situations/Crisis

Economic development does not depend only on fiscal and monetary reforms or other related macro economic adjustments in foreign trade and import and export policies. Distorted and defective political system acts as a brake and a bottleneck for achieving the goals of economic development and social justice. Economic justice demands a guarantee of work to every able bodied citizen, satisfaction of basic needs of every individual and provision of equal opportunity who wants to develop his personality. The disparities in income should not be such as to create an unbridgeable gulf between the rich and the poor. There are bound to be violent tensions, conflicts and struggles in a society which is divided into two hostile classes of the very rich and the very poor ; there shall be no harmony and spirit of fraternity in such a society. There can be no social and economic justice in society based on economic injustice and exploitation.

However, the liberal democratic Constitution of India has the Directive Principles of State Policy on the concept of social justice on the economic side which are as under :

Article-38 : (1) The state shall strive to promote the welfare of the people by securing and protecting as effectively as it may social order in which justice—social, political and economic—shall apply to all the institutions of nation life.

(2) The state shall in particular strive to minimise the inequalities in status, facilities, and opportunities, not only amongst individuals but also amongst groups of people residing in different areas engaged in different vocations.

Article-39 : The state shall in particular direct policy towards securing :

(a) That the citizens, men and women equally, have the right to an adequate means of livelihood;
(b) That the ownership and control of the material resources of the community are so distributed as best to subserve the common good;
(c) That the operation of the economic system does not result in the concentration of wealth and means of production to the common detriment.

These directives are not justiciable but it shall be the duty of the state to apply these principles in making laws for the socio-economic welfare of the people. In the end, the liberal democratic political system of India owing to the adoption of the capitalist model of modernisation since Independence has in toto failed to translate these objectives into practice and thereby unachieved economic justice. It has failed to remove the class character of justice as it sanctions and institutionalises the exploitation of the weaker/deprived masses, *dalits* and working class by the capitalists and the rich peasants/landlords and politico-administrative decision makers. A society divided into the rich and the poor is incapable of providing economic justice. Briefly, it may be said that the non-implementation of these constitutional socio-economic goals/directives during the last fifty years by the distorted/defective political system has been a major challenge to the equitable and non-exploitative economic development of the country. These have remained a mere constitutional obligation. It should be clear that these directives provide the fundamentals of good governance, and for this, the state is duty bound to implement them by legislation and positive actions and thereby to promote the quality of life of the under-privileged, deprived and vulnerable strata of society. But all this needs a strong political will of the governance to implement such socio-economic measures which may be the product of the politico-ideological commitment of the party in power. However, all the liberal parties in power since Independence have lacked such commitment.

During the last decade, the Indian economy registered an average growth rate of 5.23 per cent per annum. However, the explosive growth in government expending resulting in negative savings of public expenditure and failure of the public sector to generate resources led to macro-economic crisis in the recent past. As a result, the fiscal deficit as a proportion of GDP rose from 6.4 to 9 per cent during the last ten years.[21] Fiscal discipline is still wanting.

The New Economic policy-liberalisation, privatisation globalisation in the wake of a got-up balance of payment crisis in 1991 adopted by the Indian government contradicts the Preamble provisions and constitutional socio-economic directives as well. This policy is a global integration of India with advanced industrial countries. This liberalisation policy is to foster privatisation and globalisation of the Indian economy. Liberalisation and globalisation advocate reduction of government function or less government intervention, rolling back of the state from the sphere of production and productive investment and a significant curtailment of the level of social expenditure and market friendly economy or marketisation of government functions and public services, resulting in creation of a "Police State" and maximisation of profits and competition and export led industrialisation to encourage foreign investment and technology, shifting from state led development.[22] It is, thus, obvious that the New Economy Policy (liberalisation, privatisation and globalisation) is a blow to the sovereignty of the Indian people in the economic affairs, did not produce genuine economic growth with equity and social justice and Structural-Adjustment Programme (SAP) has attacked the conditions of life and work of the working people, and poor marginalising women in various aspects of their existence.

Apart from, the liberalised/privatised and globalised economic reforms based on serious social inequalities have contributed to the crisis of governance such as the mounting burden of administrative expenditure, and of public debt; the increasing poverty (387 million 1992-93), heavy cuts in food and fertilizer subsidies, increase in food prices to an extent of nearly 11 per cent annually during the Eighth Plan period, stagnating agricultural output say declining agriculture production, foodgrains production, industrial production and generation of electricity increasing unequal competition (and acquisition spree of multinational corporations) which has led to the closure of nearly half million small scale units; domestic industries facing problem of competing with the multi-national industrial giants; increasing unemployment/underemployment; the gradual withdrawal of the government from the task of building up of infrastructure; the increasing withdrawal of the government even from its primary responsibility of providing primary education and primary health facilities. Fifty years into our life in the Republic, we find that justice—social, political and economic—remains an unrealised dreams for millions of our fellow citizens. The benefits of the economic growth are yet to reach them. India has one of the world's largest reservoirs of technical persons but also the largest number of illiterates; the world's largest middle class, but also the largest number of people below the poverty line and the largest number of children suffering from malnutrition. There has been a large number of suicides by the farmers of Andhra Pradesh, Karnataka and Maharashtra. 1.8 lakh villages still do not have a school within a distance of one kilometre how are primary school children expected to learn to be even barely literate. Water is a basic need and fundamental right of the people. Yet today; millions of the Indian masses are struggling to get adequate drinking water. As regards unemployment, between 1994 and 1998, the number of registered job-seekers with the employment exchanges went up from 3,65,00,000 to 4,11,00,000, an increase of 46,00,000. This does not include at least twice, if not three times the number of those who cannot be registered with the employment exchanges, either because they are not skilled workmen or because lack education. Many of these unemployed are candidates for social crime or for armed insurrection. Even Mahatma Gandhi believed that without economic equality, there could be no non-violence. This was not told by a Naxalite person but by Mahatma Gnadhi. Against the backdrop of such situations, human development must remain a distant dream.[23] There is really no scheme for generating more employment. On the contrary, the allocation for rural employment schemes has been reduced. The economic reforms have increased the disparity between the rich and the poor. The government seems to be quite callous on the plight of the poor.

In sum, to I.K. Gujral, the new economic policy has itself contributed to the crises of governance. Large flows of foreign money into the economy, despite our limited opening to the world outside have had at least four negative impacts on the Indian society. They have created new inequalities and sharpened the traditional ones, thereby lending new edges to social and political turmoil and disorder. Secondly, they have enlarged the width and depth of corruption. Thirdly, they have brought into being a flood of narcissist self-indulgence by a relatively small, but not insignificant, affluent consumer middle-class whose glittering life style has immensely sharpened the age old universal social contradictions in India. Finally, they have expanded people's expectations and aspirations for the glitters of good living without generating either enough national resource or enough national resource or enough national will to rapidly develop our vast depressed human resources, exposing to national and international limelight the gaping faultiness in our chosen models and path ways of development.[24] Corruption and misgovernance in India has deeper roots which cover both the public and private sectors. Apart from, globalisation coupled with intellectual property rights is also creating new challenge.

The Indian democratic state is bound to face a serious crisis because globalisation and liberalisation are bound to erode the popular legitimacy of the state. If the state is not perceived as an active promoter of the interests of 335 million Indians living below the poverty line, and if the Indian state cannot effectively deal with growing rural-urban social and economic divide, the democratic sanction from such state will be either withdrawn or it will be lukewarm. In a class divided society like India, the majority of the oppressed/exploited and vulnerable social groups support the state for a better future. A retreating state in India cannot remain democratic because serious social cleavages and crisis cannot be resolved by accepting the new methodology of market forces.[25] In reality, the market led economy and governance in India is anti-democracy. Because, markets are not the natural friends of people; they have to be made people friendly through government intervention. Three kinds of major state interventions in the market identified by Bhaduri and Deepak Nayyar are : (a) functional, (b) institutional and (c) strategic. Functional interventions seek to remedy market failures in so far as prices give the wrong signals. Institutional interventions seek to govern market by setting rules of the game for players in the market. Strategic interventions seek to guide the market, as these are inter linked across activities or sectors in an attempt to attain broader, long term objectives of development. In their views, the state must not abandon its efforts and dilute its role in the name of liberalisations.[26]

In other words, state regulated market and market regulated enterprise have to be a goal. Briefly, the state must not withdraw from the basic responsibilities of social welfare programmes, like food security, job guarantees, health cares and education towards the deprived and vulnerable masses and the creation of infrastructure, nor unregulated foreign investment be allowed to cause social disruption. The Indian state has to be actively involved in the total process of production and equitable distribution and this is the only method to promote real social sector as well as to bring about economic development : This can be only possible by the state led and community based participative development instead of market led development. But the liberal Indian governance has to rectify inherited social and economic inequalities.

As the fact remains true, capitalism is developing in India in a conscious manner and state is its promoter because the capitalists are controlling the Indian governance through a variety of linkages and alliances. Hence, the constitutional socio-economic goals are unlikely to become reality so long as the present policy framework remains operative as has already been experienced during the last fifty years of Independence. The benefits of planned development in the existing socio-politico-economic power structure or social and property relations based on capitalist lines cannot percolate to the poor/weaker/neglected/deprived sections of the Indian society. In other words, there cannot be any improvement in the life of the peripherised masses without institutional change, change in the distribution of assets and incomes in favour of the poor, which is not possible without genuine and determined political will. This in turn, depends on a change in the correlation of inter-class forces in favour of the deprived and vulnerable masses. Because, poverty question is a power question. It is rooted in the model of development the country has adopted, and the socio-economic power structure obtains in the country. The development strategy, as it may be emphasised, must not be seen as merely the formulation of a new economic strategy/policy. It has to be concerned with all the different dimensions of social and property relations in India today. Even the political restructuring of the present political system has to be considered.

Administrative Challenge/Malaise and Corrective Measures

In relatively backward countries, the liberal democratic political system propagates the values of liberty and equality. It generates a lot of hopes on the minds of socially and economically deprived/poor/vulnerable sections. But these hopes are soon belied because liberal democracy remains what Michael Parenti calls, "Democracy for the Few". This failure often alienates people from liberal democratic political system. The Indian liberal democratic state is not exception to this rule. The alienation of the people from the Indian governance during the post-Independence period has become evident in the wake of social, political and economic conflicts and strong public protests arising out of non-operationalisation of constitutional socio-economic goals and grossly repressive measures to contain such conflicts and protests.

The systematic denigration of the constitutional institutions, collective failure to protect and uphold the Constitution by its custodians viz. politico-bureaucratic class and the alienation of the people from the liberal democratic governance of India owing to the distinction between the constitutional goals and operational goals being paradoxical have been a serious/major concern as regards the mal-administration in India. Timely decisive intervention in several matters of vital constitutional and national importance has been sadly lacking. No wonder, when the Constitution itself has been thrown to winds, the country's policy and, consequently, the administration is in such mess. It is, thus, not the Constitution, but its faulty implementation, which has one of the root causes of the present day ills/mess.

The liberal democratic state of India has pursued the capitalist model of development and capitalist social and property relations after Independence. In 1991, the government has further pursued the new economic policy (liberalisation, privatisation and globalisation) market economy framework or market led development emphasizing the state to retreat or to minimise its role. As a consequence, the Directive Principles of State Policy cannot be achieved by a retreating state. All these policies, which have been in the operation since Independence, have widened/sharpened disparities between the rich and the poor, frustration, estrangement, deprivation, exploitation, poverty, insecurity, oppression, land alienation/agrarian social conflicts, dependency, threats of starvation and injustices of all sorts. This capitalist model of development/market led development also leads to uneven development, regional economic imbalances and conflicts and tensions of all sorts, affecting internal security adversely. The liberal democratic state of India has failed to introduce a complete decentralisation in social, political and economic spheres resulting in social vacuum that leads to social/class conflicts. No effective land reforms, highly corruptive election system, influenced by money and muscle power/rigging, using castes/ communities as vote banks, criminalisation of politics and politicisation of bureaucracy—rise of mafias, mastan, speculators, black marketeers, smugglers, unholy nexus among politicians, bureaucrats and criminals/industrialists, corruption in public administration/public life are serious threats to the foundation of the Indian governance. India today is among the poorest countries of the world with the largest number of illiterates and at the same time, it is considered to be one of the ten most corrupt countries of the world. Rise of fundamentalism, communalism ethnic regional identity problems, linking of religion with politics, decline and disintegration of political parties, non-responsive, rigid and frigid administration and highly proliferating non-performance bureaucracy with little accountability, increasing interference in the working of constitutional and administrative institutions and forces responsible for maintaining law and order, disregard for rule of law and Human Rights by the custodians of the liberal democratic Constitution of India, social movements, insurgency, terrorism, communal riots, organized forms of violence supported by political parties/political masters/rich and external and internal divisive/disruptive forces, no accountability of the elected representatives, no transparency in the governance, collapsing of judicial system in which to obtain justice becomes difficult, expensive for the poor, overdelayed and frustrating, and poor or low or biased performance of the state have definitely weakened the democratic legitimacy of the Indian governance. Politico-administrative system in the country also lacks integrity, moral values and determined will and has become insensitive to people's problems. As George Fernandes has rightly said, 'looking at the way we dedicate ourselves to eradicate poverty, whether while in the government or in the opposition, it seems to me that there is vested interest in preserving poverty. Creating an enlightened and equitable society would deprive the elite who have held the reins of governance whether as permanent government-bureaucrats or as an elected government, or for that matter, as military dictators, the permanent right to rule'.[27] Thus, the Indian administration is witnessing a serious crisis because its economic, political and moral order is in turmoil mainly owing to the pursuit of the new agenda/ policy by the Indian ruling/elite class which is anti-development. anti-government and anti-sovereignty. In reality, the market led development and governance based on capitalist lines are contrary to the democratic Constitution of India.

The problems confronting the Indian governance which are arising out of the failures of the nation-building, need to be responded with a determined political will and administrative conviction by the politico-administrative system. A major structural shift and institutional change in the existing socio-economic model of development on capitalist lines, exploitative social and property relations and the pursuit of the new economic policy or market economy framework are suggested. The positive role of the state in resolving social, political and economic conflicts/problems seriously-affecting the Indian masses living below the poverty line adversely is emphasised. Retreating state as desired by the new economic policy. (liberalisation, privatisation and globalisation) is not required. The Indian state/political systems needs to be redesigned.

Honest and corruption free governance in this country being a capitalist oriented, class divided and an acquisitive society appears to be a distant dream. Till private property remains the symbol and status of powers, the desire to acquire it by any means remains preponderant among the individuals. The desire of the rich to become richer makes them blind to any value pattern. It is not the poverty, but the desire/greed to be rich in a capitalist society is the root cause of the evils, dishonesty, unethical behaviour and corruption. So to have an honest, corruption free and justice oriented governance is the creation of new social order based on social ownership of property, equitable distribution, fairplay and justice (social, political and economic).[28]

Poverty and unemployment questions are a power questions rooted in the development model, the Indian state has adopted and the socio-economic power structure that obtains in the country. Both have been increasing since Independence. The eradication of poverty and unemployment, an economic malady and social curse constituting a great liability to social stability depends on the restructuring socio-economic power structure, human relationships and state intervention and not on the retreating state. Employment is created under the government/public sector and not under the private sector. The government must ensure job guarantees and alleviation of poverty. Briefly, the western development model and new economic package of policies have a jobless growth and cannot alleviate poverty. Because, the benefits of the planned development in the existing policies cannot percolate to the poor/weaker/ neglected/deprived sections of the society. As a result, the weaker/ and deprived/vulnerable sections will be deprived of the development programmes but in most cases, also be kept out of the development process.

Weber's type of bureaucracy with its in-built impersonality, inflexibility and hierarchical structures, which has been functioning during the last more than fifty years, is unsuitable to the requirements of socio-economic development of the poor masses. C.P. Bhambhri's comment on the anti-democratic development role of Indian bureaucracy is relevant that the higher echelons of Indian bureaucracy were always integrated with the Indian capitalist classes. Indian bureaucracy believes in the fundamental social institution of "Private Property" and it has actively participated in managing state capitalist sector in India and it has facilitated the promotion of private corporate sector in India.[29] He has further added that the New Economic Policy has been projected within the country on the plank of "debureaucratisation" of India. Bureaucratic power never dies. It expands in every regime and assumes "relative autonomy" of its own especially in the name of management of crisis of the Indian state. Bureaucracy in India has not vacated its power space in the so called new regime of deregulation of the Indian economy. On the contrary, it has increased its powers because of its global connections and by championing the cause of transnationalisation of Indian market economy.[30] Mohit Bhattacharya has also expressed a similar view that the bureaucracy in India–the top–administrators, the armed forces and the law and order machinery is the objective manifestation of the inequity creating apparatus of the state. The role of bureaucracy is subsumed in the over arching character.[31] However, bureaucracy as a form of organisation is a fit agency for stability and conservation, and not for change and development. It is not necessarily bad. What is needed, is a transformed bureaucracy called development socially responsive bureaucracy for which proper training and motivation are the primary needs. Organisational adjustment to make a close fit between development needs and organisational format is needed. It is further suggested to debureaucratize and not "unbureaucratize" by means of decentralisation, people's participation and placing reliance on civil society/voluntary organisations and other people's autonomous efforts. Besides, goal and result oriented administration and people/poor oriented approach less of rule of law and process are the primary needs.

Police force in democracy should be under the control of politically elected leader which ensure accountability of the police force. The central and the state governments have not made a distinction between the causes and symptoms of social unrest. While police can deal with the symptoms—a riot, it is beyond its power to root out the causes that spark it off. Police can intervene to maintain law and order but it neither revolves the basic contentious issues nor be substitute for government to resolve fundamental social conflicts. For, example, agrarian conflicts are product of landlord and land relationships. So agrarian conflicts have to be resolved by attacking the root cause of rural poverty and unemployment and by restructuring the landlord and landless relationships. Communal divide cannot be responded by police. It has to be politically responded by cementing majority and minority relationships. Police intervention in social conflicts must not be permitted. Police also needs to be democratised.

Election laws and procedures need to be reformed. Criminals, mafias, chargesheeters and those involving in scams/corruptions (whether convicted or cases pending against them in judicial courts for decisions) must be debarred from contesting elections. To curb money power, a complete ban on donations by big Business Houses/ companies to political parties in the present context of clandestine political deals in multicrore financial scams of diverse sorts must be made.

Adherence to the constitutional socio-economic goals/ provisions and commitment to their implementation especially in favour of the poor/*dalits*/deprived/exploited/vulnerable sections of the society by the public servants have to be taken care of or emphasized. Here is a worth to take note of the President K.R. Narayanan's observations that we have to consider whether it is the Constitution that has failed us or whether it is we, who have failed the Constitution.[32]

Accountability of the elected representatives to the electorates/ voters/ and also the system of Recall of the elected representatives by the electors are to be considered, if by his performance in or outside the legislature, he has lost their trust. This will discourage political defections and split. People are important, not the selfish politicians. The government has to look to latter for the survival of the former.

REFERENCES

1. Bhambhri, G.P. *Indian Politics since Independence*, New Delhi, Shipra Publications, 1994, pp. 349-351.
2. Mukhopadhyay, Ashok. Reinventing Government for Good Governance (in) the *Indian Journal of Public Administration* (Special Number on Towards Good Governance) *Quarterly Journal of IIPA*, July-September, 1998, Vol. XLIV No. 3, New Delhi, p. 281.
3. Minocha, O.P. *Governance in an Era of Turbulence* (in) Souvenir of Indian Institute of Public Administration, Delhi Regional Branch, New Delhi, August, 1998.
4. *Ibid.*
5. *Ibid.*
6. Gujral, I.K. *Crisis of Governance* (in) *Mainstream* (Weekly) Vol. XXXVIII , No. 18, 22 April, 2000, New Delhi, p. 8.
7. *Ibi.*, p. 8.
8. *Ibid.*, p. 8.
9. *Ibid.*, p. 9.
10. Venkataraman, R., Perspective of Good Governance (in) *Mainstream* (Annual Issue – 1999), December 25, 1999, New Delhi, p. 16.
11. Dubey, Muchkund. National Must Heed the President's Warning (in) *Mainstream*, Vol. XXXVIII, No. 16, 8 April, 2000, New Delhi, p. 7.

12. *Ibid.*, p. 9.
13. Prasad, R.N., National Agenda of the New Government : Administrative Dimensions – An Appraisal (in) Administrative Review, *Annual Journal of Indian Institute of Public Administration*, Mizoram Regional Branch 1996-1997 (issues), p. 104.
14. Bhambhri, C.P., *The Indian State : Fifty Years*, Delhi, Shipra Publications, 1997, p. 162.
15. Bhambhri, C.P., *Politics in India – 1991-92*, Delhi, Shipra Publications, 1992, p. 237.
16. Bhambhri, C.P., *op cit.*, p. 175.
17. Bhambhri, C.P., *Ibid.*, pp. 175-76.
18. Rathore, L.S., Political Culture of India's ruling Class, (Presidential address was delivered by him at XII Rajasthan Political Science Assòciation, December 4-5, 1989) p. 11.
19. Rathore, L.S., *Ibid.*, p. 14.
20. Bhambhri, C.P., *op. cit.* p. 176.
21. Minocha, O.P., *op. cit.*
22. Prasad, R.N., Our Goals for Twentyfirst Century : (a) Economic, (b) Social and (c) Administrative. Some Suggestions (in) Administrative Review, *Annual Journal of IIPA*, Mizoram, Regional Branch, (1996-1997) issues, p. 91
23. Fernandes, George., Essence of Human Development— Equity with Economic Growth (in) *Mainstream*, Vol. XXXVIIII, No. 24 of June 3, 2000, New Delhi, pp. 8-9.
24. Gujral, I.K., Governance of India, (in) *Mainstream*, Vol. XXXVIII No. 34, August 14, 1999, p.10.
25. Bhambhri, G.P., *op. cit.*, pp. 198-99.
26. Bhattacharya, Mohit., Rolling Back the State: Public Administration in The Age of Market Supremacy (in) *The Indian Journal of Public Administration* (Special Number) Vol. XLII, No. 3, July-September, 1996, (*Quarterly Journal of IIPA*), p. 256.
27. Fernandes, George., *op. cit.*, p. 9.
28. Prasad, R.N., National Agenda of the New Government : Administrative Dimensions – An Appraisal (in) Administrative Review, *Annual Journal of IIPA*, Mizoram Regional Branch (1996-97- issues), p. 100.
29. Bhambhri, C.P., *op. cit.* (14), p. 219.
30. *Ibid.*, p. 227.
31. Bhattacharya, Mohit., *Development Administration*, New Delhi, Jawahar Publishers, 1997, p. 23.
32. Narayanan, K.R., Placing Accountability over Stability (in) *Mainstream*, Vol. XXXVIII, No. 8, February 12, 2000, p. 10.

2

CONFLICTS ARISING OUT OF CONTRADICTIONS IN INDIAN POLITICAL SYSTEM

Their Implications for Internal Security

Contradiction and conflict are two very close in meaning but there is a considerable difference between the two Contradiction and conflict are often generated in the liberal political system having classes and based on capitalist model of development. Liberal politics is an effort to bring about the rule of order and justice in which power guarantees the general interests and common good against the pressure of private interest. To Marxists, politics is a conflict, a struggle in which power allows those who possess it to ensure their hold on society and to profit by it. So the terms "conflict", "contradiction" and "political system" are of central importance which need to be understood.

In the liberal view of political system, "conflict" exists in terms of problems which need to be solved. Conflict does not, or need not run very deep; that it can be managed by the exercise of reason, goodwill, and a readiness to compromise and agree. On this view, politics, is not civil war conducted by other means but a constant process of bargaining and accommodation, on the basis of accepted procedures, and between parties who decide as a preliminary that they want to live together more or less harmoniously. This sort of conflict is not injurious to society but it has positive advantages. It is not only civilized, but also civilizing. It is not only a means of resolving problems in a peaceful way, but also of producing new ideas, ensuring progress, achieving ever greater harmony. Conflict is functional, a stabilizing rather than a disruptive force.

The Marxist approach to conflict is very different. It is not a matter of problems to be solved but of a state of domination and subjection to be ended by a total transformation of the conditions which give rise to it. Conflict, no doubt, may be attenuated, but only because the ruling class is able by one means or another — coercion, concessions, or persuasion to prevent the subordinate classes from seeking emancipation. Ultimately, stability is not a matter of reason but a force. The antagonists are irreconcilable and the notion of genuine harmony is a deception or a delusion, at least in relation to class societies. Briefly, contradictions inherent in the structures are the primary cause for conflicts and collective behaviour manifestations in the form of direct action, strikes and even riots.

"Contradiction" refers to discrepancy or inconsistency between two or more structures or sub-structures involving in any social or political system. It also refers to relationship between fundamentally antagonistic systems or forces, the ultimate resolution of which is possible only through a revolutionary process of conflict and change. To Marxists, contradiction is absolute, universal, and basic to nature and human society. It exists in the process of development of all things and that is the process of development of each thing, a movement of opposite exists from beginning to end. Changes in social system are chiefly due to the development of internal contradiction in society, that is the contradiction between the productive forces and relations of production, the contradiction between classes, and the contradiction between the old and the new; it is the development of these contradictions that pushes society forward.

The term "political system" has now become increasingly common in the titles of texts and monographs in the field of comparative politics/government. The concept of "political system" has acquired wide currency/use because it directs our attention to the entire scope of political activities within a society, regardless of where in the society such activities may be located. Traditionally, political science is defined as the science of the state. It is supposed to begin with the state and end with the state. In recent times, however, we find that political science increasingly uses the term 'political system' rather than the term state. The use of the new term political system is not a mere change of words. It represents a new approach, a new way of looking at the political phenomena. It not only covers the working of the state but also covers other activities and processes which hitherto were not considered to be parts of politics.

A system is a set of relationships based on some common foundation. A political system is a set of political relationships, which have a political foundation. An economic system consists of economic relationships, a social system comprises social relationships. The parts of a system are related to one-another. Where one part of the system changes, it affects the other parts as well as the whole system. In a political system, the emergence of new elements like mass political parties or media of mass communication changes, the performance of other parts also affects the general capabilities of the system as a whole.

A political system is a set of inter-relationships through which binding policy decisions are made. The association of political system with legitimate coercion in society is its distinctive feature, which demarcates it from other systems. A political system is associated with, power, rule and authority. Only the political authorities have the generally accepted right to use coercion and to command obedience. A political system includes all the interactions which affect the use or threat of use of force. It includes not only governmental institutions like legislatures, courts and administrative agencies, but all associations in their political aspect like caste groups, community organisations, phenomena like strikes/demonstrations and riots and organisations like political parties, interest/pressure groups and media of communication.

A political system is a combination of various functions, for example, that of voters, legislators, administrators, judges, tax payers, subjects, citizens etc. Besides, it has the three most important functions such as rule making, rule application and rule adjudication. In modern times, the boundaries of a political system are expanding; in other words, the functions of government are expanding. Briefly, a political system is the legitimate, order maintaining or transforming system in the society. Legitimate force is the thread that runs through the inputs and outputs of political system, giving its special quality and salience and its coherence as a system.

Structural Contradictions of Indian Political System

In relatively backward countries, the liberal democratic political system propogates the values of liberty and equality, it generates a lot of hopes on the minds of socially and economically deprived sections. But these hopes are soon belied because liberal democracy remains what Michael Parenti calls, 'Democracy For the Few'. This failure often alienates people from liberal democratic system. Indian democratic state is not exception to this rule : The alienation of the people from the government in the post-Independent India has become evident in the wake of violent social conflicts and strong public protests arising out of grossly repressive/oppressive measures to contain such protests.

The liberal democratic political system of India based on capitalist path of development and constitutionalism suiting to capitalist society has many inherent contradictions which breed a variety of conflicting situations and interests/protests. Briefly, the liberal democratic and constitutional state of India has failed to find appropriate solutions to growing conflicts of all sorts in the country and has used excessive repression/suppression to deal with social, political and economic demands of various groups in society. In short, the distinction between the constitutional ideas and operational goals is paradoxical.

Society is a web of social relationships. Society is changing. There should be a balance and harmony in social relationships. The factor which maintains balance and creates harmony is justice. Injustice means disharmony and lack of balance in society. This leads to social tensions, conflicts, struggles and protests. So, to keep society in harmony and to ensure social progress in right direction, social relationships should be on the principle of justice. Nothing is more grudged and hated than injustice. This explains why the framers of the Constitution of India declared in the preamble itself that the state shall secure to all its citizens justice—social, economic and political.

Economic Justice

It demands a guarantee of work to every able bodied citizen, satisfaction of basic needs of every individual and provision of equal opportunity to every individual who wants to develop his personality. The disparities in income should not be such as to create an unbridgeable gulf between the rich and the poor. There are bound to be violent tensions, conflicts and struggles in a society which is divided into two hostile classes of the very rich and the very poor; there shall be no harmony or spirit of fraternity in such a society. There can be no social justice in society based on the principle of injustice and exploitation.

However, the liberal democratic Constitution of India has some Directive Principles on the concept of social justice on the economic side, which are stated:

Article 38: (1) The state shall strive to promote the welfare of the people by securing and protecting as effectively as it may a social order in which justice—social, political and economic—shall inform all the institutions of national life.

(2) The state shall in particular strive to minimise the inequalities in income and endeavour to eliminate inequalities in status, facilities and opportunities, not only amongst individuals but also amongst groups of people residing in different areas or engaged in different vocations.

Article 39: The state shall in particular direct its policy towards securing:

(a) That the citizen, men and women equally have the right to an adequate means of livelihood.
(b) That the ownership and control of the material resources of the community are so distributed as best to subserve the common good; and
(c) That the operation of the economic system does not result in the concentration of wealth and means of production to the common detriment.

These directives are not justiciable but it shall be the duty of the state to apply these principles in making laws. In the end, the liberal democratic political system of India has in *toto* failed to translate these objectives into practice and thereby not achieved economic justice mainly owing to the adoption of the capitalist model of modernisation since Independence. It has failed to remove the class character of justice as it sanctions and institutionalises the exploitation of the working class by the owners of capital – the capitalist class. A society divided into the rich and the poor is incapable of providing economic justice. Further New Economic Policy liberalisation/privatisation/globalisation – market friendly economy, GATT Agreement adopted by the Indian government recently contradicts these constitutional directives resulting in less government. Thus, India is a society of unequals which materialises our upper class, vulgarises our middle class and brutalises our lower class.

Political Justice

In the field of politics, justice means equality before law, enjoyment of civil liberties, equality of opportunity; competitive politics and popular participation. These provisions are already inserted in Chapter III on the Fundamental Rights of the Constitution in its articles 14 to 22. To these articles, the state should not distinguish between citizen and citizen on the basis of caste or religion, give any preferential treatment on the basis of religion. Rule of law with independent and impartial judiciary as a protector of Fundamental Rights should be guaranteed. Basic freedoms like freedom of speech, expression, criticism, freedom to hold meetings and organise parties, freedom of press should be guaranteed. Freedom is thus corner stone of any concept of justice. Closed societies which deny freedom to individuals, also deny social justice. Political justice postulates a universal availability of the mechanism for resolving conflicting claims of different interests in society.

No doubt, the Indian political systems has all the ingredients of social justice in its political aspect. But the wide powers of executive—emergency proclamation, Preventive Detention Act, TADA Act, and many restrictions are threat to freedom. Besides, political justice appears to be meaningless especially for the deprived and vulnerable Indian masses for want of economic justice.

Social Justice

Social Justice means social equality, implying a social system where there are no special rights, no special privileges and no special dignities attached to a person on the basis of birth or caste. All have an equal opportunity to stand up and develop their personality. It implies the absence of all distinctions in the social status of the people because of difference in race, class, caste and birth. In order to break the vicious caste culture and provide social justice to all, the Constitution of India has incorporated certain provisions in the chapters on Fundamental Rights and the Directive Principles of State Policy to provide social justice to the people at large:

(i) Prohibition of discrimination on ground of religion,race, caste, sex or birth (Article 15).
(ii) Equality of opportunity in matters of employment (Artical 16).
(iii) Abolition of untouchability (Article 17).
(iv) Prohibition of traffic in human beings and forced labour (Article 23).
(v) Protection of the interests of the minorities (Article 29).
(vi) State to secure a social order for the promotion of welfare of the people (Article 38).
(vii) Provision for just and human conditions of work and maternity relief (Article 42).
(viii) Duty of the state to raise the level of nutrition and standard of living and to improve public health (Article 47).

However, social justice cannot be forced upon the people by the Constitution and the laws of the state. But more important is the change in social values, social attitudes and social institutions to achieve social justice. The basic thing is education. Education should create a spirit of enquiry in the minds of the people. It should create a power of questioning the validity of social traditions and social institutions.

As regards the achievement of social justice in India, it cannot be achieved due to India being a capitalist oriented, class divided, caste ridden and multi-religious society. Division of society into different classes being a feature of the capitalist society is a barrier to social justice.

2. Provisions of the Preamble to the Indian Constitution – sovereign, socialist, secular, liberty, equality and fraternity.

The word 'socialist' is vague and irrelevant. India has never been a socialist state. The Indian political system has been building up a capitalist oriented society instead of socialism since Independence which gives rise to social, political and economic conflicts/tensions. New Economic Policy (liberalisation/globalisation/privatisation – market friendly economy, GATT Agreement) introduced in 1991. New Labour policy (golden shake hand, exist policy), New Social Policy (more percentage of reservations/facilities to BCS/OBCS but less investment on social development) and New Administrative Policy (deregulation, delicensing, but use of para military forces and TADA Act) contradict the preamble provisions. Further the capitalist state in India based on class, caste and religious divisions cannot have a secular society, a spirit of fraternity as well as assure of the vulnerable and the very poor sections of Indian society, liberty, equality and dignity. Briefly, a multi-religious society cannot have democratic and federal state without secularism. Secularism cannot be possible if secular politicians and secular bureaucrats are not managing it.

3. Fundamental Rights only provide political rights to the Indian masses which become meaningless/useless for the disadvantaged people and the weaker sections of the Indian society. These rights do not give economic rights to the Indian masses which contradict the provisions of both the preamble to the Constitution and the Directive Principles of the State Policy, resulting in gross inequalities in property which can neither ensure liberty nor equality, nor justice. Justice is a gift of harmonious society. Property divides society and according to Madison it is the only durable source of faction. There is no justice for poor and underprivileged in a society of unequals. Laski says about economic security that where there is rich and

poor, educated and uneducated, there is always a relation of master and servant. This also contradicts the provisions of Article 46 which ensures to promote the economic interests of the weaker sections of the people (SC/ST) as well as to protect them from social injustice and all forms of exploitation.

Therefore, it is emphasised that if the liberal democratic political system of India is to succeed, the system must be backed by social and economic democracy. For economic democracy/justice, economic relations are to be suitably transformed or reordering human relations in the economic sphere between the rich and the poor to eliminate exploitation of the vulnerable sections of society has to be made.

4. Non-implementation of the provision of Article 39(a) which states that the state shall secure that the operation of legal system promotes justice on the basis of equal opportunity and shall in particular provide free legal aid by suitable legislation or schemes to ensure that opportunities for securing justice are not denied to any citizen by reason of economic or other disabilities. This directive has been added by the Constitution (42nd Aemendment Act, 1976), in order to ensure equal justice which has been promised to all citizens by the preamble, and to further the guarantee of equality before the law (Article 14) which was unmeaning to a poor man so long as he was unable to pay for his legal advisor.

5. Participation of workers in management of Industry [article 43 (A)] that the state shall take steps by suitable legislation to secure the participation of workers in the management of undertakings/ establishments, or other organisation engaged in any industry. The concrete economic result of this would be that the workers would no longer be hired labourers but shall have an interest in the success of the enterprise and would have a share in its profits. However, this provision has not yet been translated into practice which makes a strained relations between the owner of capital (capitalist) and the workers on the issue of living wages and conditions of work/ other facilities resulting in strikes, lockout, demonstrations, gheraos, hartals and processions and other violent conflicting situations, affecting production adversely. Briefly, all this leads to labour-management confontation .

6. Education system in India is in a very bad shape. Today with the exception of some of the South Asian countries India has the highest rate of illiteracy in the world. It is estimated that at the turn of this century, over 90 per cent of the world's illiterates would be living in the Indian sub-continent and most of them in India. This is inspite of the fact that Article 45 of the Constitution provides that the state shall endeavour to provide within a period of ten years from the commencement of the Constitution, for free and compulsory education for all children until they attain the age of fourteen years.

That 10 years period was over in 1960. And yet 40 years after that, more than 90 million children of school going age in India are not going to any school.

Article 46 of the Indian Constitution provides that the state shall promote with special care the educational interest of weaker sections of the people, and in particular of the scheduled castes and scheduled tribes.

Inspite of this obligation assumed by the state, there is little evidence of the equalisation of the educational opportunity in our grossly unequal society. In fact, the gap in the educational opportunity is widening. The highest incidence of illiteracy is still among these weaker sections of society. Women and the girls have the least educational opportunities in India. There cannot be any hope for achieving an egalitarian educational structure in India unless vastly expanded and improved educational opportunities are provided for these groups. Myron Weiner in his article published in the *Economic and Political Weekly* writes.

> Deep class/caste divisions have been barriers to the development of national drive for mass education by those who have made it to the upper strata. It will take a major coalition of locally based groups, active participation of media, the contribution of researchers, the support of investors, educators, social activists and trade unions to get India to address the way it treats the children of poor.

It is now universally recognised that education is both means as well as the end result of development. It is one of the basic needs of the people and their human right. Article 41 of the Indian Constitution enjoins upon the state to "make effective provision for ensuring the right to education". And finally education is the most powerful instrument for the empowerment of the people.

But the New Education Policy of the Indian government under the Structural Adjustment Programme imposed by the World Bank/ IMF emphasises science, computer, professional and Management education through private institutions which contradicts these constitutional provisions.

7. Centralised federation generates a lot of conflicts/tensions, cieavage between the central government and state governments. So, some state governments have persistently demanded a re-examination of the constitutional provisions regarding the distribution of powers between the centre and states. Because the federalists want powers for the state governments to meet the growing demands of the people for economic development and social transformation. India is a country of regional imbalances and diversities and such imbalances can be corrected only if the state governments have adequate financial and legislative powers to respond to the specific challenges of development. Federalism is based on balance of powers and this is possible to achieve if empirical reality is kept in mind. The economic development for the whole nation cannot take place without strong state governments. However, the Constitution has itself visualised a strong centre and the challenges of times have only made it doubly important. These new dimensions of Indian Federation are the product of centralised planning, the dependence of the states on the centre for finance, and the dominance of the political party at the centre and in almost all the states. Even when different parties come in power at the centre and the state government (irrespective of party considerations) will have to accept the policy decisions of the central government in the field of economic planning due to financial sanctions of the centres. (B) Non-implementation of Sarkaria Commission Report (Centre – State relations).

To Construct a new federal balance in India, the present centralised federation may be changed into a co-operative and constructive federal polity. Four measures are suggested :

(i) Territorial reorganisation of states on the basis of their being socio-culturally homogeneous and administratively and politically manageable.

(ii) Amendment to the Constitution of greater administrative and fiscal powers to the states for effective socio-economic development and political stability.

(iii) Activisation of the Panchayati Raj and Nagarpalika systems with necessary devolution of authority to build active grassroot democracy by implementing the Constitutional Seventy Third and Seventy. Fourth Amendment Acts relating to PRIS and Nagarpalika.

(iv) Building of a new federal consensus – between parties, social activist groups and citizens to fight communalism, casteism and separatism and to defend the values of democracy, secular polity; federal nation-building and social justice.

8. Frequent use/misuse of the constitutional provisions of Article 356—Emergency Powers over the years has definitely shifted this balance in favour of the Central Government. Briefly, in the Indian federal set-up, the Central Government is very strong and it has many over-riding powers over the state governments. The Constitution visualizes four types of crisis, when the Central Government might intervene or even take over legislative and executive powers/control of any state (i) security of the country or any part of it is threatened by war or external aggression or by an armed rebellion, (ii) Breakdown of constitutional machinery in a state, (iii) Financial stability of the country, of one or more states threatened, (iv) External agression and internal disturbances under Article 355 to ensure that every state government is carried on in accordance with the constitutional provisions.

Since 1960, article 356 has been invoked for over one hundred to dismiss the popularly elected governments, covering all the states at one time or the other, at times when there was absolutely no justification to do so on grounds of threat to security or the failure of the constitutional machinery. In recent years, whenever a conflict arose between upholding the spirit of democracy and federalism and the interests of the ruling party, invariably the decision was in favour of the latter.

In the 17 years from 1950 to 1967, the president's rule under article 356 was imposed only on 9 occasions. In contrast, in the four years from 1967 to 1971, when the Congress party under Mrs. Indira Gandhi reemerged as the dominant party, President's rule was imposed 11 times. Thus, the response of the Central Government is dictated by partisan political considerations than the question of constitutional propriety or situation.

Before dismissing a state government, by the centre, all possible steps including issuing warning to the state governments to improve matters by the centre are suggested.

There is a need to rethink of the role of the President, when the basic features of the Constitution, its democratic and federal character are being undermined by the decisions of the council of Ministers.

In a pluralistic society like India, emergency powers are essential, but it has to be ensured that the 1975 type emergency situation is not repeated.

The role and powers of the governors and their advisors need to be clearly spelt out. Governors should be provided with an "Instrument of Instructions" under the Constitution so that they cannot function in partisan manner.

As governors have a key role to play during emergency situations, whenever a state government is dismissed, some norms should be laid down about the appointment of governors. Governor's office is increasingly becoming politicised. They are expected by the ruling party at the centre to be their agents rather than independent constitutional authority. The recent appointment of Romesh Bhandari as the UP governor shows that things have not yet changed even during the present UF Government which is never short of rhetoric to emphasize its democratic credentials.

The security problems which necessitated the inclusion of emergency powers in the Constitution have not eased. They may have multiplied. The secessionist forces have become more powerful and violent and are being actively supported by anti-national forces from both inside and outside the country. Society is getting increasingly polarised on religious, caste, linguistic and regional identities. Social, political and economic conflicts are becoming more violent. The policing of borders with Pakistan, and even with Nepal, Myanmar and Bangladesh has become a major problems. The threat to India's security, integrity, sovereignty and stability is more serious today that at any other time during the post-independence period.

The fact is that President's rule has not always been a model of good governance. On the contrary, it has been both unpopular and inefficient. Actually, it functions more according to the pulls and pressures of the ruling party at the centre. It gives rise to many extra constitutional centres of power which do not hesitate to manipulate the government to serve their vested interests/narrow ends.

Therefore, the emergency powers are essential, but there is also need to introduce effective check so that these cannot be easily misused. In the end, impartiality and independence in politics is essential if the governor is to perform his constitutional responsibility with decorum and dignity.

9. Western model of development administration along capitalist line-emphasising growth that is jobless, ruthless, voiceless, rootless and futureless. These five types of distortions have been identified by the United Nations Human Development Report, 1996 (HDR) that can afflict the growth process both in developed and developing countries.

The features of growth are disturbing. Jobless growth means, the overall economy grows but does not expand the opportunities for employment – (which is what has happened in India). Ruthless growth stands for a situation where the fruits of economic growth mostly benefit the rich, leaving millions of people struggling in ever deepening poverty that phenomena is occurring in India. Voiceless growth means where growth in the economy has not been accompanied by an extension of democracy or people's empowerment including gender empowerment. Rootless growth means where material growth/prosperity is achieved but people's cultural, social and ethnic identities are to wither – This phenomenon too is visible in India – North-East). Futureless growth is environment unfriendly, where the present generation squanders resources needed by future generations. This is happening at a large scale in India. In short, this capitalist model of development leads to uneven development, regional economic imbalances, a larger number of people to live below the poverty line, unemployment and all sorts of conflicts/tensions, affecting, internal security adversely. This development model contradicts the socialist and economic provisions of Directive Principles of State Policy.

In the third world, democratic decentralisation has long been regarded as a necessary condition of social, political and economic development. But the democratic state of India has failed to introduce a complete decentralisation in social, political and economic spheres resulting in social vacuum that leads to social/class conflicts.

10. No effective land reforms all over the country being the most dominant factor in the rural power structure have been undertaken so far except West Bengal, Tripura and Kerala which generate agrarian unrest/problems/conflicts and the landless poor peasants and the landlords implicating for internal security problems.

11. Highly corrupt election system, influenced by money and muscle power using castes/communities as vote banks.

12. Criminalizing of politics – rise of goondas, mafias, mastan, speculators, black marketeers and smugglers, unholy nexus among politicians, bureaucrats and criminals/industrialists.

13. Corruption in public administration/public life in India.

India today is among the poorest countries of the world with the largest number of illiterates and at the same time it is considered to be one of the ten most corrupt countries of the world.

To tackle corruption, the realization of the need for rigorous standards of honesty must come to those who are occupying higher echelons of power because corruption percolates from them to the lower strata also. Till private property remains the symbol of status and power, the desire to acquire it by any means remains preponderant among the individuals. In an acquisitive society, the desire of the rich to become richer make them blind to any value pattern. It is not poverty, but the desire to be rich in a capitalist society that is the root cause of the evil; and the permanent solution of the problem is the creation of new social order based on social ownership of property, equitable distribution, fair play and justice.

14. Rise of fundamentalism, communalism, ethnic, regional identity problems and linking of religion with politics, Nationality question, theory of the son of the soil.

15. Decline and disintegration of political parties, growth of pressure groups. Not ensuring inner-democracy in every party/body/ organisation/society/association/union which is registered or recognised.

16. A reacting non-responsive rigid and frigid administration and highly proliferating bureaucracy with little accountability – Non-performance of bureaucracy.

17. Consistent undermining of the constitutional and statutory bodies, ensuring necessary autonomy to enable them to discharge their duties/obligations.

18. Not creating quasi-judicial bodies in every statutory organisation to regularly and constantly resolve the organisational conflicts.

19. Not creating effective public grievance redressal cell at all levels.

20. Collapsing of judicial system in which obtaining of justice has become too difficult, expensive for the poor, over delayed and frustrating.

21. Incessant and increasing political interference in the working of administrative institutions and forces responsible for maintaining law and order.

22. Disregard for Rule of law and Human Rights by police/ forces, excesses committed by police and paramilitary forces, not creating of permanent/regular Human Rights Protection Commissions at all levels.

23. Problem of unemployment/under employment.

24. Social movements, insurgency, secessionism/ militancy, terrorism, communal riots, organised forms of violence supported by political parties/political masters/ the rich and external and internal divisive/disruptive forces.

25. No accountability of the elected representatives because of big social distance between the elected representatives and the

electorate. The mass of voters have no direct relationship with their elected representatives.

26. Poor or low or biased performance of the state has definitely weakened the democratic legitimacy of the state. Gunnar Myrdal in his book the *Asian Drama* has characterised India as a "soft" state because of its incapacity to restructure social relations in the face of the powerful social groups. Our analysis is that India is a "vulnerable" state because a large section of society feels that it has been marginalised by policies of neglect by the state.

Implications for Internal Security

India has evolved a unique state system which is based on democratic participation, federal arrangements of governance and secular and socially accommodation process of modernisation. Every pillar of this system is in deep crisis and the state functionaries are making fundamental compromises on every basic social goal of the state. A system collapses when the state functionaries do not struggle to uphold the basic values or when they fail to apply appropriate correctives to restructure the state. The erstwhile USSR and Yugoslavia have been obliterated from the world map because the leaders of these countries failed to rectify serious distortions of their systems. Similarly in India many fundamental steps have to be taken to face the emerging multi-dimensional challenges and conflicts arising out of the distortions of the political system and thereby affecting internal security adversely if the country wants to move forward on the basis of democratic, federal and secular system.

Owing to the distortions of the Indian political system as well as the non-translation of the constitutional goals and socio-politico-economic provisions into practice for the socio-economic transformation of the wretched conditions of the underprivileged and deprived sections of the Indian society, the violent/coercive public protests in the forms *of hartals,* boycotts, strikes/lockouts, fasts of political nature, civil disobedience movements, gheraos and other forms of direct action, communal riots/tensions, social and political movements/violence, uprising/insurgency, ethnic upsurge and agrarian social conflicts/tensions, terrorism etc. persist.

Although the Indian state has built up a powerful police system to deal with uprising/insurgency, secessionism, communal riots/ tensions, social and political movements, terrorism and agrarian social conflicts and other forms of internal disturbances/disorders, the country continues to be torn by strifes. In Punjab, Jammu and Kashmir, Assam, Tripura, Manipur, Nagaland, Andhra Pradesh and Bihar, terrorism/insurgency/uprising and other socio-economic movements/tensions rage on. Undeterred by the strong police presence, agrarian conflicts/unrest continue to rock rural India particularly Bihar and Andhra Pradesh. The Indian liberal democratic state has not learnt any lesson from the failures of the police to contain social, political and economic conflicts in the country. The Central and State Governments have not made a distinction between the causes and symptoms of social unrest. While police can deal with the symptoms – a riot – it is beyond its power to root out the causes that spark it off.

The police is active in fighting against social conflicts, because political masters/politicians have abandoned their role of resolving the conflicts through political means. Briefly, the governments (centre/state) have failed to come to terms with seminal causes of social tensions/conflicts. If this trend is not reversed, India will cease to be democracy and it will become a full-fledged police state. Already parts of India have become a police state and democracy has ceased to function in Punjab, Kashmir and north-eastern states. Even in the states with democratically elected governments, the police is active and overshadows democratically elected leaders when it comes to dealing with social challenges. In short, the police can intervene to maintain law and order but it neither resolves the basic contentious issues nor be a substitute for government policies to resolve fundamental social conflicts.

For example, agrarian and social conflicts are products of landlord and land relationships. So agrarian unrest has to be resolved by attacking the root causes of rural poverty and unemployment and by restructuring the landlord and landless relationship.

Insurgency/secessionism/terrorism cannot be contained by the illegalities of the police. Communal divide cannot be responded by the police. Insurgency/secessionism/socio-politico-economic movements etc. have to be politically responded by following the strategies of accommodative pluralist and federal nationalism. Communal divide has to be politically responded by cementing majority-minority relationships. In the absence of a political agenda, politicians have taken recourse to hand over the problems to the police. Its implication is very clear. Police is demanding its pound of flesh. It wants manpower increase and modernisation of its weaponry. It also wants a free hand in dealing with insurgency, agrarian unrest, terrorism, naxalism and riots etc.

Police forces in democracy should be under full control of politically elected leaders. This is the only mechanism to ensure accountability of the police forces. Police indulges inillegality, if it is not accountable to the elected representatives of the people. Police has to play a legitimate role in every society but it has to be controlled and held leash by the law of the land.

Politicians in India have contributed to the growth of lawlessness of the police. First the politicians have abetted and supported the police functionaries to employ illegal methods to perform illegal tasks for their political and personal/partisan purposes. Second, during abnormal time, politicians abdicts their responsibility and hand over the conflict situations to the police.

Briefly the police cannot be allowed to substitute democratic politics. Police interventions in social conflicts have shown their limitations.

The Police, thus, being a part of the Indian political system often commit excesses and illegalities while ensuring law and order, and dealing with the sensitive issues of communal riots, social conflicts and safeguard of Human Rights as alleged by many commissions of inquiry. The fact is that all these unconstitutional and illegal deals of the police/security forces are contradictory/ negative generating conflicts of many types which are no doubt, implication for internal security.

With a view to contain conflicts of all sorts, positive efforts to remove contradictions inherent in the political system have to be taken by the political masters with conviction and determined political will. But as the fact remains true, the benefits of the planned development in the existing socio-politico-economic power structure cannot percolate to the weaker and neglected/deprived sections of the society. So, the socio-politico economic power structure and property relations, generating large scale disparities in the Indian society have to be radically restructured, otherwise the weaker/deprived sections will not only be deprived of the development programmes but in most of the cases, they will be kept out of the development process. Because poverty question is a power question. It is rooted in the model of development, the country has adopted, and the socio-economic structure that obtains in the country. What I want to emphasise is that the development strategy must not be seen as merely the formulation of a new economic strategy. It has to be concerned with all the different dimensions of social relations in India today. Even the political restructuring of the present political system has to be considered. The perspective has to be of involving the people in the solution of their own problems. It is also sure that with planned modernisation based on the principles of "distributive justice" and 'democratic socialist arrangement', the conflicting situations/social movements will get weaker and the forces of peace and egalitarian values stronger in the long run. Thus, the multiple challenges of nation building can be met only on the basis of uniform national policies and the basic struggle in India is not to deconcentrate or fragment power but to create political power which can lead the nation and defend the vulnerable strata of society. The need of the hour is, goal oriented politics to build national economy, implement national policies and create appropriate administrative and political institutions for the mobilisation of the national effort to achieve growth with equity and social justice.

3

PROSPECTS OF COALITION GOVERNMENT IN INDIA

Coalition Politics in India is a direct legacy of the period of one party dominance (Congress). The party had a monopoly of power both at the centre and the states. But after the Fourth General Elections in 1967, the Congress Party's monopoly of power came to an end due to its omissions and commissions, centralised and authoritative administration and inherent contradictions. Nine states had non-Congress governments. Briefly, there had been the Congress's precarious hold both at the centre and the states. The end of the Congress Party's monopoly of power greatly helped the emergence of an effective multiparty system, giving birth to coalition government in the country.

The term "Coalition" is derived from the Latin word *Coalito* which is the verbal substantive of coalescere. 'Co' means 'together' and 'alescere' means 'to go, or 'to go together.' The meaning of coalition according to the dictionary is an act of coalescing or uniting into one body, a union of persons, states or an alliance. It is a combination of a body or parts into one whole. The term "Coalition" as is generally used in political science, has gained currency out of the exigencies of a multiparty system in a democratic setup. It is a phenomenon of a multiparty government where a number of minority parties join hands for the purpose of running of government, which is otherwise not possible in a democracy based on majority party system. A coalition is formed when many splinter groups in the House agree to join hands on a common platform by sinking their broad differences and cobble a majority in the House. It is an astonishing chorus of discord. Though outwardly a coalition appears to be one solid mass, inwardly, it is ridden by party foibles and frantic party fervour and bickerings and it is for this reason that coalitions prove to be transient. According to F.A. Ogg "the term 'coalition' as employed in a political sense, commonly denotes a co-operative arrangement under which distinct political parties unite to form a government or ministry".

Basically there are two types of coalition theory–the first, power maximization theories and the second, policy based theories of coalition formation and behaviour. Power maximization theories stress the maximization of pay offs, that is power and derivatives as the key factor in the coalition formation, ignoring ideological and policy affinities as factors. Policy based theories, on the other hand, consider such affinities the key to the formation of coalitions power maximization theories, accordingly, predict minimum winning coalitions defined as a coalition in which each party is indispensable to the coalition's winning a simple majority of seats because in such coalitions, each member's share of the pay off is maximized.

Policy based theories predict minimum connected winning coalitions. That is, coalitions that are composed of member parties adjacent on the ideological scale and at least not incompatible on major issues, thus minimizing the ideological range and within this limiting condition the minimum member of parties needed for a majority. Empirical evidence from the comparative literature on coalition politics tends to support policy based theories and hence the importance of compatibility for coalition formation and even more for coalition longevity. About two-thirds of majority coalitions in the developed countries in the postwar period have been ideologically connected. This is so especially in most European politics and in Israel where there are clear ideological and social divisions and where parties identified with particular ideological positions and social constituents have fairly stable support base. However, within these constraints, pay off maximization plays powerful behavioural role.

After the setback of the Congress party in many federating units of the country since 1967, some of the then Congress Union

Ministers and some other politicians have been advocating the presidential form of Government of India by replacing the Parliamentary form of government with a view to ensuring continuous and coherent leadership, stability as well as strengthening the Centre's authority to counter the divisive forces in the country, resisting impulsive popular pressures and strong regional aspirations in the interests of national unity. The strained and uncooperative centre-state relations are also factors for coalition government leading to a demand of the Presidential system. Undoubtedly, the Presidential form of government represents a type of representative democracy. In contrast to Parliamentary government, its feature is that the elected President and the Governor through electoral college holds office whether or not they are supported by the majority of the legislators, the elections can be managed by the government.

Parliamentary form of government means government by consent or public criticism, ensuring election by popular vote and those who want majority rule and majority wishes to prevail and also to satisfy legitimate aspirations of the people, must stand for the parliamentary form of government over the Presidential. In the current political scene, the presidential form of government may easily degenerate into army dictatorship or totalitarian/autocratic governance that must be avoided at all costs. The framers of the Constitution have also rejected the American model of the Presidential system. What is required is a frank recognition of the changed political reality to make parliamentary democracy more meaningful. Country's regional, cultural, ethnic and lingual diversities do not permit to adopt the presidential system. Briefly, to seek unity and diversity in the country will be hampered by the adoption of the presidential form of government.

To constitute a National Government as suggested by some seasoned politicians in a parliamentary democracy with multiparty system having divergent, heterogeneous, regional views/opinions/ policies/programmes and subjective considerations/personalised politics appears to be impracticable in a country like ours. Besides, there may be a problem for nominating the right/up right elected members of the national government by the President who lacks faith in the preamble to the Constitution of India—democracy, secularism and socialism; though the market economy adopted by the Government of India contradicts the preamble provision – "socialism". Above all, the Constitution has no provision of National Government. If the President is empowered by having such provision in the Constitution, the President is bound to indulge in Party Politics and personalised politics. All this needs structural shifts which are unsuitable to Parliamentary Democracy meaning a party rule. Therefore, the existing constitutional arrangement is better suiting that the President should exercise his tact, wisdom, objective/impartial considerations in having an alternative and stable government keeping in view the established conventions.

The present political scenario is the outcome of centralised and authoritative administration and leadership in our federal system in the past (Nehru-Gandhi-Rao era). The behaviour of the political parties has much to do with the recent massive structural shifts in the political, economic and ideological spheres of the Indian society. Rapid expansion of market, extraordinary growth of communications and infotech, new industrialization and globalization are throwing up new social strata. At the same time, they have added new vigour to the traditional groupings of various classes, castes, and communities, the downtrodden social groups have become more vocal and active. The new middle class and working class sections have come into being and there is a considerable increase in the activities of the new small entrepreneurial classes. All this is reflected in the constant changes in the various political parties, formation of political groupings, increased factions and defection within the national parties and constant unprincipled shift in the policies of the parties. The most important aspects is the main conflict between secularism and communalism. This has demanded a unity of all secular forces however, loose and ill-defined. It would be unrealistic to ignore these new realities. Owing to the plurality of the Indian society, social and culture heterogeneity and diversities in terms of classes, castes religions and regions and other reasons mentioned above, helping the growth of competitive multiparty system, it appears that minority governments and coalition government have come to stay in contemporary political situation though the coalition governments both at the central and state levels since 1967 were formed but the models of coalition politics except in West Bengal, Kerala and Tripura was a complete failure due to narrow selfish gains, vested interests, factions and defections, horse-trading, personalised politics, clash on personality cult and the lack of fair play among the coalition partners.

The 1996 Parliamentary Elections

But the 1996 elections to the Lok Sabha were unique and historical as none of the political party or pre-poll combination of political parties (BJP, Congress and National Front-Left Front) could get a majority in the Lok Sabha. The much trumpted dominance of the Congress Party on the Indian political scene ignominiously ended. The verdict reflected a four fold division of the people's preferences; one, the Bharatiya Janata Party (BJP) emerged a single largest party securing 161 members and with its allies Shiv Sena (13), Samata Party (8) and Haryana Vikas Party (3), it demonstrated an impressive tally of 187. Akali Dal won 8 seats in Punjab and decided to support BJP in the formation of government. Second, the Congress Party won 140 seats even less than what it got in 1977 in the Janata wave. Third, National Front-Left Front combine is also loser in the elections. The Janata Dal secured 44 seats, Samajwadi Party, an ally of Janata Dal got 16 seats, making a total of 60 seats which the Janata Dal alone obtained in the 1991 Parliamentary elections. Similarly, in the Left Front, the CPI (M) Seats have been reduced from 37 to 32, CPI's from 14 to 13, the forward Block remained constant at 3 while RSP has added one seat taking its tally to 5. Presently, the National Front-Left Front combine has 112 members in the Lok Sabha having its presence only in 11 states. Fourth, the various regional political parties performed very well. The DMK won 17 seats, the Telegu Desam (TDP) 16 seats, the Tamil Manila Congress (TMC) 20 seats, the Asam Gana Parishad (AGP) 5 seats, the Indian National Congress, INC(T) 4 seats, in the elections adding to the strength of 65 supported by 12 members of other political parties. Thus the verdict shows that India is not a monolith.

The President invited Atal Behari Vajpayee, the leader of the single largest party (BJP) to form the Ministry and also asked him to prove majority support to the government on the floor of Lok Sabha by May 31, 1996. He was sworn in as Prime Minister on 15 May, 1996. He resigned on 27 May, 1996 without trying the strength of his Ministry on the floor of the Lok Sabha.

National Front-Left Front combination persuaded the secular forces to unite against the communal forces (BJP and its allies) and thereby floated a united front of regional political parties such as TMC, DMK, TDP, AGP, INC(T) supported by 12 members of other smaller parties. All these take the strength of 190 at par with that of BJP group. The 13 parties united front formed the coalition government headed by H.D. Deve Gowda, the Janata Leader as the Prime Minister, the Congress Party and the CPI(M) supported the government unconditionally from outside. It may be here kept in mind that the Congress party's support to the United Front Coalition government is a sudden and unique historical development. it is also reported that the major cause for the United Front formation is to ensure a secular state, guarantee social justice and equality to the minorities and to prevent BJP from coming to power as it is a communal party. As the United Front government depends on the support of the Congress(I), it is believed that the policies of the Congress(I) have to be generally pursued by the United Front government without major changes. It is also important to note that a Federal Front comprising regional parties (DMK, TMC, TDP, AGP etc.) was formed after elections which played a very active role in the formation of the United Front government. For the first time, the regional parties joined the United Front Government at the Centre to share their responsibility and thereby to participate in the decision-making process. The Federal Front was formed to achieve a true Federal Indian State with strong states, strong centre and mutual strengthening. So, the government should attempt to meet popular aspirations for better governance.

Prospects of Coalition Government

If a coalition government has to function successfully, the following observations/suggestions may be taken into consideration :

1. Coalition politics/system based on pre-elections alliances of political parties with similar political orientations and ideological consensus/harmony may succeed and be stable. This may be possible with left parties only. Because the basis of their coalitions is democracy, secularism, social justice and economic equity. For instance, coalition governments in Kerala, West Bengal and Tripura have become regular feature of Indian polity and these models have earned reputation.
2. Coalitions of pre-election alliances of national and regional political parties with divergent and heterogeneous policies/ programmes based on an agreed minimum socio-economic programmes to be executed with strong will and determination in coordinated directions may function. But, the government policy should be consensual and the group would not be at the whim and fancy of one leader, taking adhoc and arbitrary decisions. But the combination should come out with a platform for secular democratic alternative based on social justice and economic equity.
3. Post-election coalition is a system of power-shating between coalition partners based on the number of seats won by the parties in their respective states. Such coalition governments were led by V.P. Singh and Chandra Shekhar and 13 Parties (National and Regional) United Front Coalition government led by H.D. Deve Gowda, this coalition spectrum from the left to the Congress is based on an agreed common minimum programme and also reflecting a socio-economic political reality in which no single policy and ideology dominates.
4. The realities of political governance of social and economic situation demands a concrete approach rather than blind criticism. The parties are increasingly realising that the questions of democracy, secularism, social justice, economic equity and new Indian needs demand mutual consultation and dialogue rather than head on collisions.

Coalition partners agreement to a power-sharing formula and

Prime Minister by rotation for the smooth functioning of such coalitions is suggested. Because the regional leaders representing geographically demarcated power bases constitute this inter-party coalition, the potential Prime Ministers are to be chosen from amongst them (regional leaders) securing the largest number of seats. If it were two, then for 30 months each, if three, then for 20 months each.

Once the two or three Prime Minister designates agree upon, it is better to follow the British system in which the Prime Minister does not hold a portfolio and devotes his time to leading the country with the assistance of his cabinet colleagues. The portfolios can be shared within the parties in order of their performance. For example, Home, Finance and External Affairs portfolios, which are considered weighty, would be claimed by more powerful parties and the others would have to be content with textiles, ocean development and the like.

Joint leadership, thus, reflects the plurality of political strength, federal in nature, closer to the people and better equipped to avoid the pitfalls, heavy handed central rule. This system would finish off the Delhi zamindari, the leaders, who have no power base and who do their politics through the media. The game of the most political parties is the rootless politician, who has little connection with the people and has no idea about the needs and aspirations of anyone other than himself.

Such a system of power-sharing between coalition partners would have something for all the partners and although there is always scope for discontent. There is also a chance that such a system of sharing power and the perks of office could work. It is in any case worth trying. It cannot be a greater disaster than the eleventh months of disputations and disoriented governance that a similar combine delivered in 1989.

Power-sharing is not a new concept. It has been tried in various forms with quite a lot of success in many smaller countries with lesser ethnic and regional diversities than that of India. Israel offers an example of successful power-sharing and a Prime Minister by rotation Israel had a coalition Government of the Likud party and the Labour party from 1984 to 1988. For the first two years Shimon

Peres was the Prime Minister and Yitzhak Shamir, the Foreign Minister and for the next two years, roles were reversed. Despite their widely different backgrounds and political perceptions, Shimon Peres and Yitzhak Shamir ruled in the best interest of Israel. Germany is another country which has developed the concept of power-sharing to an advanced degree. After 1957 when Government had a single majority government and the Christian Democrats were in power, there has always been a coalition Government in Bonn. The Government coalitions have been of different compositions in the states and at the centre since 1957 but they have almost always worked.

The game of the most political parties is the rootless politician, who has little connection with the people and has no idea about the needs and aspirations of anyone other than himself.

While entering into a coalition after the election, the coalition partners in Germany enter into a coalition contract. Once the coalition contract is in place, however, there is no adhocism about governance and bearing exceptions, no major disputes. The coalition contract lays the broad thrust that the government will take. It contains an agreement on all the laws that will be legislated during the period. This system ensures that despite political differences between coalition partners, the country has a stable government that provides coherent administration and leadership.

Switzerland has also institutionalised coalition system. It is a plural society like India where political parties represent the interest of the three major language groups (French, German and Italian) and the two religions (Catholic and Protestants) It is a tradition there for the four largest parties to come together after the elections and form a coalition.

5. The Constitution is silent on what the President should do if no party is in a position to command a majority in the House. The President's goal is to get a viable government and that he should be free to call any person who in his opinion is able to provide for country. The Sarkaria Commission while laying down guidelines for the Governors in the choice of the party for forming the government, said, a combination of parties which

is able to command a majority in the House, he should be given the next opportunity calling parties in order of their strength in the House will certainly be the most prudent and non-controversial course of action.

In 1989, the Congress was defeated in the pools but it had the largest membership in the Lok Sabha. Rajiv Gandhi did not stake his claim to form the Government. The President R. Venkataraman following the British precedent called on the next party Janata Dal in order of strength headed by V.P. Singh to form the Government. Again in 1991 when no party had a majority in the Lok sabha, the President invited the leader of the then largest single party the Congress and on his acceptance of responsibility appointed him as the Prime Minister. The President R. Venkataraman suggests that a convention be established by President and Government to follow the practice of inviting parties according to their strength adopted in 1989 and 1991 by the President. So, this is a grey area where a well defined convention on the line of the British convention should be established sooner or later either by Judicial interpretation or by a political consensus in the areas where the Constitution is silent.

6. The political leaders of the coalition system want to survive by disrupting and disintegrating various parties by encouraging political defections and splits in political parties in the country. These are an expression of the ills of our economy and of a democratic behaviour of the people in any economically backward area and have to find their expression through individual defections. There will be no solution to the problems of splits and defections unless we conclusively solve our unending economic, political and social problems. There is no reasonable remedy to these problems under the present Constitution. The Constitution does not also provide for the recall of a legislators in the event of his defecting from the party on whose ticket he has been elected. So a system of recall of legislators to discourage political defections and splits is suggested. Besides, the electors should be empowered to recall their representatives if by his performance in or outside

the legislature he has lost their trust. Now, such a provision cannot be included because of cumbersome procedures involving a heavy burden on the exchequer and unreasonable expectations from the illiterate voters.

7. The ploarisation of political parties is neither supported nor the replacement of the parliamentary system by any other means be suggested. Any of the steps which later has to be undemocratic even remotely must be shunted. Either two party system or three party system in not only feasible in such a vast country as ours but is also not efficacious for the growth of its diverse cultures which we want to nourish. The accommodation of divergent political opinions is possible only under a system that is not opposed to multiplicity of parties. The Constitution also allows these cultures and opinions a full play. We also seek unity in diversity. So harping on democracy as well as on crushing political opinion is either illogical or nothing short of hypocracy. Since elections in India have failed to democratize politics in its true sense, there is need to change the concept of elections to canalise the multiparty system into desirable directions. The only course left with us is the multi-party legislatures with a near proportional representation to each party commensurate with the number of votes cast in its favour.

The President R. Venkataraman suggests that a convention be established by President and Governors to follow the practice of inviting parties according to their strength adopted in 1989 and 1991 by the President.

8. The present system has encouraged confrontationist politics. So, the politics of confrontation is to be replaced by consensual politics on a secure-basis. Besides, it is also experienced that parties may have majority of electorate behind them but they cannot run the government because they have not obtained majority of seats in the Lower House/Assembly. Proportional representation seems to be remedy. It will strengthen party discipline and legitimate make that party rule which has obtained

majority of votes in the elections. The government should represent the majority of voters. Any party or combination of parties, which have received more than 50 per cent of the votes polled, should be given the right to get the Lower House and assembly dissolved. Party discipline will increase in the system of proportional representation. A party should have a right to expel a member (who is elected on that party ticket), if he wishes to leave the party. If there is a direct co-relationship between the percentage of votes polled and party strength in the House, it will be more democratic than the present system. Majority principle is the quintessence of democracy as established in India. Proportional representation re-establishes the importance of votes and the role of political parties.

9. Dissolution of the House should be a device to resolve an acute political crisis in a country or a state.
10. The stability of a coalition government depends on the policies/principles guiding its formation and its cohesion and capacity for democratic decision-making. A truly representative coalition should reflect the trends expressed in the elections. Besides, when different parties enter into coalitions, they must necessarily downplay their differences and give up all their majority criticisms, no matter how grave these might be. Briefly, consensus politics is the need of the hour.
11. The consensual style of the working of the Prime Minister of the coalition government may ensure longevity in office. The Prime Minister is not supposed to bypass the decisións of his Council of Ministers, knowing the fact that the coalition government is different from running a one party rule government. The Prime Minister should have a certain talent for keeping his team together. These should be more consultations and consensus or mutual discussions. This culture of running the government with common sense approach to problems, collegiate type of functioning, coordinated effort, and collective decision has to be evolved.
12. The coalition government has to strengthen the key institutions of federal government through the consensual style.

Constitutional authorities, institutions/arrangements must be allowed to function. Bureaucracy, while controlling it should be allowed to perform the duties. It may be noted that people are more important, not the selfish politicians. So, the U.F. coalition government has to look to the latter for the survival of the former. The present government has to take care of the continuation of economic reforms with social justice, growth and equity.

Lastly, it is true that in many parts of the world, it has been established that one dominant party rule need not always be equated with stability. Nor should coalition governments be equated with instability. It is possible to have a stable and credible government under a coalition, based on an agreed Common Programmes executed with Will and Determination to keep the nation politically stable, socially harmonious and economically vibrant. Those in search of stability must bear in mind this lesson of history which is quite relevant to India's present situation.

Not only this, but India has entered a phase of coalitional politics. It appears that coalition will be a natural phenomenon in India in the years to come. The reality of a "Hung Parliament" has ushered in a new era of coalition politics. The crisis of Indian polity in recent times is that structurally there is no one party or combinations of parties that would provide a stable and progressive government. In order to meet this challenge, Indian polity should learn how to organize a system of government that will enhance the level of people's participation in a highly diver and plural society. Coalition of convenience will not endure as it will promote political instability in India. Political instability in states has a constitutional cure the form of imposition of President's rule. But there is no constitutional cure for political instability at the centre. The only remedy is political readiness of political parties to subscribe to coalition politics. Indian political system has to evolve the culture of a coalition government. The 1996 Lok Sabha elections have left the political parties and groups with no choice but to evolve workable formulation of governance. The imperatives of coalition politics have to be recognised and accepted by all political parties. It is also relevant to conclude with Narasimha Rao, the former Prime Minister, who said at Behrampur on 20th June, 1996 that the time has come to learn how we can work unitedly. He went on to term, the Deve Gowda Government as one of the strongest governments whose fall he cannot visualise.

REFERENCES

Abraham, A.S., "Coalition Politics : Federal System is Inevitable" *The Times of India*, Patna, 29 May, 1996.

——, A weekly Journal *Mainstream*, New Delhi, (All issues of 1996).

Bhambhri, C.P., "Coalition and Governance" *The Hindustan Times*, Patna, 31 May, 1996.

Chakraborty, Nikhil, "Coalition Compulsions, *The Hindu*, 27 July, 1996.

Dodd, Lawrance G., *Coalition in Parliamentary Government,* Princeton University Press, 1976.

Gadgil, V.N., "Coalition Politics Congress must stay out" *The Times of India*, Patna, 13 July, 1996.

Gehlot, N.S., Coalition Politics in India : A Critical Analysis, paper presented at Member's Annual Conference of IIPA, New Delhi, 1996.

Gupta, Dipankar, "Coalition Politics : Making a Virtue of Necessity. The *Times of India*, 26 June, 1996.

Limaye, Madhu, Coalition Politics — Fairplay is pre-condition, *The Times of India*, 23 May, 1996.

Minocha, O.P., *Coalition Government : Experience and Prospects,* theme paper presented at members. Annual Conference of the Indian Institute of Public Administration, New Delhi, 27th October, 1996.

Ogg. F.A., "Coalition" in *Encyclopaedia of the Social Science,* New York, 1957.

Prasad, R.N., *Coalition Government in India : A Study of its Prospects,* Paper presented at Prelude Seminar on IIPA, New Delhi Theme (1996). *Coalition Government : Experience and Prospects,* prepared by O.P. Minocha which Aizawl Local Branch of the Indian Institute of Public Administration organized on 14th October, 1996.

Rao, V. Bhaskara., Coalition Politics : Prospects of Public Administration in

India, paper presented at annual members conference of IIPA, New Delhi, 1996.

Ricker, Wiliam H., *The Theory of Political Coalition,* London, Yale University Press, 1962.

Sahni, N.C. (ed.), *Coalition Politics in India*, Jalandhar, New Academic Publishing Company, 1971.

Tiwana, S.S., *Coalition Politics in India : Problems and Prospects,* Paper presented at Member's Annual Conference of I.I.P.A, New Delhi, 1996.

4

SECULARISM IN INDIA
Problems and Perspectives

PART - I

Since the study is concerned with Secularism in India, it is necessary at the outset, to know the concept of secularism. The word secular is derived from the Latin word "Seculum" which means 'Temporal world'. George Jacob Holyoake is credited with the coinage of the word 'Secularism' used the term to denote social ethics based on natural morality, but independent of revealed religion and supernaturalism. Secularism according to the Oxford English Dictionary, means "concerns with the affairs of this world, worldly, not sacred, not monastic, not ecclesiastical or sceptical of religious truth". According to G.G. Hackman, Secularism signifies the kind of life that is lived in complete indifference to God and to religious values. In other words, secularism is neither anti-religious, nor non-religious. Secularism is neither anti-God nor pro-God. It treats alike the devout, the antigonistic and the atheist. It eliminates God from the matters of the state and ensures that no one shall be discriminated against on the ground of religion. To clarify further, it is better to mention that secularism promotes understanding, harmony and cooperation between different religious groups for national unity, entails the supremacy of state and its laws equally for all citizens, helps liberation of the civic polity from religious dominated groups and parties, and enforcement of the principles of fraternity of the citizens and not members of primordial groups—religious, linguistic, ethnic or regional. Secularism as a phenomenon in India represents a struggle for building an integrated political community in a multi-religious situation and also against the process of fragmentation of our integrity and community as a sovereign people. Secularism is the refutation of any form of theocratic culture and religious separatism and it is opposed to the domination of any church priest or any form of organised religious authority in its political culture. But it does not mean opposition to religion. It also does not mean appeasement of the minority, and it certainly, also does not mean religious dictatorship of the majority. It is simply a code of behaviour in relation to man's social and political activities independent of religion. Thus secularism with all the rationalist and humanistic values triumphs only by relegating man's religion to his personal life. Secularism cannot and does not exclude minority religion from its purview That is to say, the concept of secularism applies universally and without making an exception of any religion. Secularism requires that the citizen themselves keep their religion separate from the rights and obligations of citizenship. It, thus, stands for secular attitude in the common man. Briefly, secularism, rightly understood,, embodies a broader vision, greater inspiration and more progressive outlook than that provided by traditional religions whether of the majority or the minority. It greatly concerns for culture, social progress, improvement of the material conditions of man and economic justice to society. Secularism also envisages a political structure in which individual is not subject to any social inequities imposed by the religious sanction.

In fact, secularism is a principle of policy which aims to extricate from the traditional nets of religion everything in which the state has a vital interest from the point of political, economic and social progress.

PART - II

The secular state is one where the concept of secularism should be the accepted policy A secular state treats religion as an individual enterprise and individual action lying outside the true and legitimate province of government. It should observe scrupulous neutrality among religions and confine itself to secular objectives clearly dissociating itself from religion. Secularism is not so much a matter of state policy but an attitude, a way of life which leaves no room for intolerance and leaves each individual to develop his inner life in his own way. It is not merely the peaceful coexistence of different faiths but an affirmation of the duty of the state and its citizens to look at each individual citizen, not as a part of a group but a free normal person with his own rights.

The foundations of India are based on the democratic principles and the secular provisions in the Constitution. India is a secular state. So the state guarantees individual and corporate freedom of religion dealing with individual as a citizen irrespective of his religion. It does not promote any religion. It does not also interfere with any religion. There are people of different faiths living in India. Although there have been intermittent religious conflicts, India is secularly established as a secular state. As regards secular provisions in the Constitution for the promotion of a secular state, the liberty to worship proclaimed in the preamble to the Indian Constitution is ensured by recognising it as a Fundamental Right. There are detailed provisions in chapter III of the Constitution on Fundamental rights for securing the freedom of religion.

Article 25-29 guarantee every individual the freedom of religion to profess, practise and propagate his own religion without interference and at the same time assume strict impartiality of the state and its institutions towards all religions. The secular nature of the state has been further emphasised by inserting the word in the Preamble to the Constitution by the Forty Second Amendment. Article 25 further adds that all persons within the jurisdiction of the Republic, whether national or foreigners, are equally entitled to freedom of conscience and the right to freely profess, practice and propagate religion. But this right is subject to two limitations. This right cannot be misused to contravene public order, morality, health, and other provisions of the Fundamental Rights. This right does not prevent the state from making any law regulating or restricting any economic, financial or political or other secular activity which may be associated with the practice of that religion. Nor does it restrict the right of the state to legislate for social welfare and reform or for throwing open Hindu, Sikh, Jain institutions of a public character to all classes and sections of the people professing these religions. The court has the right to determine whether a particular right or observance is regarded as essential by the tenets of a particular religion.

Article 26 of the Constitution also guarantees to each person and every section the right to establish and maintain institutions for religious purposes, to conduct his or its own affairs in religious matters, to own and acquire movable and immovable property and to administer such property in accordance with the law. Religious property enjoys tax concessions. To article 28, no religious instructions shall be imparted in any educational institution other than those under an endowment.

It further restricts the right of the state to religious instructions and lays down that no student attending any educational institution recognised by the state or receiving monetary aid from the states shall take part in any religious instructions or to attend any religious worship without his/her consent.

Thus every person has the right to hold any faith of his choice. Every group has also the right to preach the aims of its religion. But the Supreme Court has held that the right to spread does not give any one the right to convert people of other faiths by such means, fraud, inducement or allurement.

PART - III

The freedom of conscience and religion enshrined in the Constitution prohibits discrimination on ground of religion, caste, sex and place of birth. But this right does not prevent the state from making any special provision for the advancement of any socially and educationally backward classes of citizens or for the scheduled castes and scheduled tribes. Article 16 further guarantees every individual that freedom of equal opportunity in the matter of employment or office under the state. So the state is prohibited to discriminate on grounds of religion, race, caste, sex and place of birth in the matter of employment. But sub-clause 3 of Article 16 does not prevent the state from making any provision to reserve appointment or posts for any backward class of citizens, who are not represented adequately in the state services. This provision may be called protective discrimination to correct the traditional inequalities. Thus according to Nehru and Constitutional law experts like Prof. Alexandrowiez, the discrimination is meant to protect the interests of certain backward and depressed classes. Further no individual is discriminated to have access to public places, places of worship and admission to any educational institution maintained or aided by the state and the right to vote. Article 17 forbids the practice of untouchability in any form, to give effect to this fundamental right, the enactment of the untouchability (offences) Act, 1955 under Article 17 of the Constitution is the greatest achievement in abolishing the age-long practice of Hindu religious custom of untouchability which is against the fundamental rights of the citizens that all are equal and also is against the principle of welfare state. Secularism is, thus, essentially a practical approach for maintaining social stability and harmony.

The Constitution also protects the cultural and educational rights of religious and other minorities. Articles 29 and 30 safeguard the right of the religious and other minorities to have a distinct language, script and culture of their own, and to establish and administer educational institutions of their choice. But the state cannot impose on them any culture other than the communities' own culture. Also no individual can be denied admission to state maintained and aided educational institution on the basis of religion, caste, sex and language. The state in granting aid, shall not discriminate against any educational institution managed by a minority whether based on religion or language. To Article 30 (1), if the state acquires the property of a minority educational institution, full compensation has to be paid.

The commitment of the secular state has to provide secular law to the citizens as well as to play active role in secularising society. While the idea of the secular state implies secular law, it also contains a conception of freedom of religion which for many present day Hindus and Muslims has a direct bearing on the continuance of their respective religious laws. But this obligation of Indian Secular State has been served by Article 44 of the Directive Principles of State Policy and accordingly, the state must endeavour to secure for the citizens a uniform civil code throughout the territory of India. In fact, important areas of civil law, including marriage, divorce, inheritance, succession, all remain under the religious personal laws. But India is committed by its Constitution (Article 44) to the elimination of this system of personal law for the sake of promoting secularism and democracy to an extent. But in this context, the enactment of the Muslim Women (Protection of Rights on Divorce) Bill to override the Supreme Court judgement in the Shah Bano case by the Rajiv Gandhi government in 1986 was a severe setback to secularism and democracy.

Since India has a multi-religious society, the country provides for each citizen the fullest freedom in religious faith and worship, and ensures good relations among various religious minority groups and promotes not only religious tolerance, mutual respect and accommodation of dissent but also reverence for all religions so that the people understand each other better and live amicably together. Indian Secularism opposing to narrow orthodox and fanatical religious views also encourages people to stress on truth, goodness, justice, fair play, and moral uplift. Because, there is no religion higher than truth and righteousness. The secularist policy of the government also means that all individuals in political, economic and social matters irrespective of their religious beliefs and other distinctions, enjoy equality of rights.

PART - IV

Seeing the happenings caused by a decline of democracy in the country today, it is almost impossible to be very optimistic about the future of secularism in the country. Despite the Constitutional safeguards in favour of secular commitment, a fundamentalist and militant communalism, casteism and ethnicism generated by the Old British game of 'divide and rule' continue to raise its ugly head from time to time, trying to fragment the national identity as well as to plaque the political system. There are also some aberrations in the Indian Political System namely, populism, economism, parachialism, and the breakdown of the national consensus, which stand out as severe impediments in the process of socio-economic transformation and secularisation. Not only but politics has become the hand-maid of hooligans, muscleman, money power, flattery, blackmail, cheating, bribing, pandering to the beast of communalism and ethnicism. To grab and retain power in their hands and in the hands of their families and friends have become the supreme consideration of politicians. Hence, the politics of vote, with all its corollary, determine all policies and actions. What better method, there can be to monopolise power than to keep the divisions of society into various castes, classes and communities on a mutually fighting pasture and then exploit their fears, susceptibilities and ambitions? To the misfortune of the secularisation in the country, the vested interests in all the communities and the politicians of all hues, who matter in power-politics of the country, indulge in these nefarious games and fissiparous tendencies, in varying degrees. They play dual role marked by public promises and private betrayals to remain themselves in power. Thus politics divorced from morality neither implements the secular provisions of the Constitution of India for secularising the Indian society nor finds solutions for national unity. As a result, the secular civic culture has not been fully internalised by all sections of the Indian society.

The existing socio-economic structure based on the capitalist path of modernisation/development that the country has adopted after independence, have sharpened not only the caste, religious, linguistic, cultural and ethnic distinctions and communal tensions, it has also increased/widened regional economic imbalances/disparities, frustration, estrangement, feeling of deprivation, socio-economic injustice, negligence and insecurity coupled with the instinct of preserving the distinct cultures and traditions among various nationalities, sub-national groups and ethnic tribal groups. The market economy framework has only helped to create a new properly tied dominant caste-cum-class forces, bereft of values which thrive on crass opportunism, partronage, nepotism and corruption, keeping the lower castes and classes outside the pale of the beneficial effect of national development and the range of national prosperity. In a situation of unequal advantage, every increase in the GNP and in national standards of living would continue to give unequal benefits to the entrenched 'haves' at the expense of the disinherited and dislocated 'have-nots', notwithstanding the slogans about democratisation, distributive justice and socialism. The fruits of economic development should reach the common poor man, because the common masses prefer economic advancement to political emancipation. This has not happened because the government has been highjacked by the politician-bureaucrat-contractor lobby, middlemen and the powerful economic strata of society. This hold of middlemen or contractors or dominant class over the government can be broken, if developmental works are transferred to local institutions. Involvement of local people in federal nation-building through local institutions is essential to deepen the concepts of both secularism and national identity. Besides, if the common poor people from oppression, deprivation, exploitation, socio-economic injustice, land alienation and dependency are to be liberated, the present socio-economic structure, which increases/permits inequality/disparity, exploitation, injustice of all sorts, oppression and emergence of propertied dominant class, has to be radically restructured or transformed. It may be also mentioned that a narrow economic approach or bureaucratic approach must give place to a new enlightened and progressive policies for bringing about the basic socio-economic changes, which will certainly contribute to secularisation, modernisation and political integration at a rapid rate. Also the ills of social injustice and economic inequality, poverty, want, unemployment, deprivation and alienation must end fast to promote secular civic culture and national solidarity

PART - V

Adherence to religious and religious system is not communalism. Exploitation of religion is communalism. Attachment to a religious community is not communalism. Using religious community against other communities and against the nation is communalism. A true believer in religion is also expected to be a good human being. But it is wrong to assume that communalist are religious people in the real sense of the word. Communalism is perversion of religion from a moral order to a temporal arrangement of a contemporary convenience, from a faith into a constituency, from a strategy of living into tactics of politics, from an end to means. Communalism exploits parts of religious dogma for expedient political purpose. It is promoted by a real or an imaginary fear of other communities. Communalism is the enemy of progress, revolution, democracy, federal nation-state building, and mono-religious state structure building.

Communalism is basically an ideology of political allegiance to a religious community as a primary and decisive group in the polity, and for political action. It is a sectarian, restrictive and negative response to the process of modernisation, and modern-nation-building. Communalism, thus, is a political strategy opposed to nationalism as an aggregation of multi-ethnic, multi-religious and multi-lingual communities. Communalism is also opposed to secularism as a pattern of socio-cultural coexistence and political integration. Communalism is opposed to a rational civic basis of party formation and political system. Communalism perceives majorities and minorities as segments and divisions within a polity and a nation, based essentially on religious communities and not even on any other ascriptive basis (like that of family, clan, tribe, caste, language, region or domicile), and certainly not on the basis of political, ideological, party, class interests or state consideration, which is the hall-mark of a modern political system. Politicisation of religious community opposed to other communities and the nation is the main plank of communalism. To attack and murder a human being in a frenzy or riot, only because he belongs to another community is the worst form of communalism. To incite communal animosity and hate by word of mouth or publication, particularly by using one's privileged position in profession and society especially the media is wicked and manifest communalism. Communalism, today, is a multi-pronged challenge which seeks to disrupt India's multi-religious fraternity It is also an affront to India's nationalist identity, and tragic set-back to evolving secular culture. It is subversive of our political stability, economic development and secularism.

PART - VI

The neglects in providing education for the children and youth leaving their minds devoid of the ideal of secularism, equality and humanism and the failures of development plans have facilitated the spread of the reactionary and divisive influences of communalism and religious fundamentalism among the people. Thus in an emerging highly technical society, neglect of education and development may promote mediocrity among the youth thereby exposing them to the reactionary forces waiting for an opportunity to spread their influence. Can any development programme hope to succeed without universalising and democratising education and decentralising the planning process? Briefly, it may be said that such communal violence is an expression of the failure of the process of nation-building. The problem of the future of secularism in India is not just a social problem of achieving a changed pattern of thought and behaviour of different people of India. It is mainly an economic problem of removing the obstacles in the path of the development of the people so that they can develop according to their own genius and culture. The perspective has to be of involving the people in the solution of their own problems. But this can be possible only by implementing land reforms. Because, giving land to landless means transferring assets to the assetless. So removing inequality in landholdings is also necessary precondition for meaningful decentralised planning.

Besides, the government, the political parties and the voluntary organisations, wedded to secularism must come together forgetting their personal bias and prejudices to work out a common agenda for action to fight the forces of communalism and fundamentalism.

Education plays a vital role in promoting democratic secular values and ensuring the unity of the people and their loyalty to the nation. So it needs to adopt an educational system bereft of all communal, religious and regional negative influences. A plan to revamp the educational system and recast it with a thrust towards unity, secularism and democracy should be drawn out by educationists, Vice-Chancellors of Universities and Heads of national educational institutes of standing. They should examine education at all levels as to impart a pronounced emphasis on democratic secular values, both in class work as well as field practices. Such an emphasis can be promoted through various social, cultural and recreational activities of the N.S.S., N.C.C., sports and culture, youth camps and inter-University meets. All sectarian and communal organisations should be disaffiliated from students' and teachers' union. The UGC should play a vital role in this regard.

The Ministry of Human Resources Development should gear all its activities to the principal role of promoting democratic secularism in the educational institutions to fight the communal and religious forces. Education policy must aim at not only inculcating scientific temperament, it must develop a sense of tolerance and feeling of oneness and nationalism in students. A short crash courses in promoting the values of secular democracy, morality, objectivity and rationality should be organised in all institutions of learning and training.

Similarly, all non-governmental youth and welfare organisations, getting support from the government, should also relate their activities to fight the communal and sectarian forces influencing the youth in the country.

Political parties wedded to secular values should come together to fight the emerging influence of communalism/fundamentalism in the country. There is an urgent need in India today to create a national front of democratic and secular forces in order to restore to the Indian state the authentic secular image, and help it to play the catalytic role as an instrument of socio-economic change, in order to change a traditional society into a modern polity.

An emphasis on the humanist tradition in all religions should be made. Because it lays stress on individual moral code, propagates the values of love and compassion in human life, and bridges understanding between diverse religious traditions, by identifying similarities of images and values, despite divergences in nomenclature. It projects the basic values of life and happiness for all, adherence to truth, goodness, justice, fairplay, toleration, mutual respect and accommodation of dissent. It speaks of God as a universal God, of religion as a humanistic endeavour, of society as a common responsibility. It points out to the futility of doctrinaire disputation and dogmatic fights, and extol the lasting benefit of the values of 'live and let live', of plurality of perception but unification of human goodness and concern for all.

Besides, the democratic and socialist appeal must have a positive content in respect of people's sense of loyalty to their language and history. On such approach, a sense of loyalty for the Indian nation can be built up and her secular character guaranteed.

In brief, Indian democracy and secularism must aim at the process of incorporating various parts of the society into a functioning whole towards the reduction of barriers between various parts of the whole, the opening of communications and ultimately the tolerance of difference within the unity, the emergence of faith in Political System and the emergence of shared values and perspectives or consensus.

At the same time, as we enter the new millennium, we citizens of India, irrespective of caste, community, religion, politics and region have a responsibility to come together to keep this nation secular. Our task is to root out the communal cancer. India cannot prosper, if the country is divided on the basis of caste, creed, beliefs or religions. Ours is a country of pluralism, of diverse cultures and people. Each of the groups—regional, linguistic, religious and social in the country have made their unique contributions to the rich legacy of India. Differences in creeds, cultures, religions and beliefs does not have to divide us. They can enrich and promote. It is the politician of the kind we have in the country who have divided us to further their own interests. The need today is to go beyond such divisions and fight for a secular and pluralist nation by uniting ourselves. We cannot progress if we allow our leaders to flaunt laws, appoint criminals as ministers and allow them to engage in communal politics by destroying churches, mosques, people and institutions. We need to make a conscious choice to come together in spite of all differences to save India. We have a duty and a responsibility to protect the rich pluralistic and secular heritage of the country Let our determination be as we have to work for the protection of the pluralistic cultural heritage of India by defeating opportunistic and communal forces and their leaders.

Despite all this, it, as a conclusion, may be noted that it appears difficult to establish secular society based on civilized, humane and just civil order without giving any reference to the existing social structure and class character of the state power in India. The capitalist state of India based on class, caste and religious divisions cannot have a secular society/spirit of fraternity and assure of the vulnerable and the very poor sections of the Indian society liberty, equality and dignity. Briefly, a multi-religious society cannot have a democratic and federal state without secularism. Secularism cannot be possible, if secular politicians and bureaucrats are not managing it. It is only democracy based on secularism which will keep India united and the other road will lead to violence and disintegration of the country. So, reordering human relations in the economic sphere between the rich and the poor to eliminate the exploitation of the disadvantaged/deprived sections of the Indian society has to be made. Besides, to construct a new federal balance in India, the present centralised federation may be changed into a cooperative and federal polity.

SELECT READINGS

Balasubramanian, M., *Nehru : A study of Secularism*, New Delhi: Uppal Publishing House, 1980.

Bhargava, G.S., Secularism and Democracy, *Mainstream*, January 30, 1993.

Gajendragadkar, P.B., Concept of Secularism, *Indian and Foreign Review*, 1 April, 1969.

Glasner, Peter F., *The Sociology of Secularisation* : A Critique of a Concept, New Delhi, Ambika Publications, 1977.

Khan, Rasheeduddin, Secularism and Social Transformation in India, I, II, III *Mainstream*, April 24, 1993; May 1, 1993; and May 8, 1993.

Gupta, Shrinivas, Nehru and Secularism, *Link*, November 17, 1991.

Mustafa, Seema, Taking Secularism to the Masses, *Mainstream*, January, 25, 1992.

Nandy, Ashis, Secularism, Seminar, June, 1992.

Patwardhan, Achyut, Secularism and the Religious Mind, *Mainstream*, August 15, 1992.

Prasad, R.N., Secualarism and Constitution of India, (Radio Talk on AIR, Aizawal).

Prasad, R.N., Role of Administration in National Integration, (Radio Talk on AIR, Aizawal).

Prasad, R.N., National Agenda of the New Government : Administrative Dimensions — An Appraisal (in) *Administrative Review*, An Annual Journal of the Indian Institute of Public Administration, Mizoram Regional Branch, Aizawal, 1996-1997 (Two Issues) (Published in 1998).

Prasad, R.N., Jawaharlal Nehru and Problem of National Integration : A Study (in) *Teaching Politics*, The Journal of the Delhi Political Science Association, Vol. XV No. l, 1989 (Department of Political Science, University of Delhi).

Rahman, A., Science and Secularism, *Mainstream*, November 14, 1992.

Seshadri, K., Nehru and Decline of Democracy, *Link*, November 17, 1991

Uniyal, Lalit, On Secularism, *Mainstream*, October 26, 1991.

5

NEW PANCHAYATI RAJ SYSTEM AND PEOPLE'S ASPIRATIONS

In order to improve the participation of the rural people in the process of their control of resources, development and involvement in decision-making and decentralised planning directly affecting their life, the Government of India has provided constitutional legitimacy/status for village Panchayats under the Constitution (Seventy Third) Amendment Act, 1992. It envisages to achieve grassroot democratic polity by making Panchayati Raj System an instrument of rural local government and community development. The Act provides reservation from women and weaker sections to ensure their participation at all levels of the Panchayati Raj Institutions. It has granted a sort of uniformity in the PRIs by making the three tier system a permanent feature. It has regularized the electoral process by making elections an imperative following the termination of the PRIs after every five years under the supervision of the State Election Commission. The provision for setting up of the State Finance Commission guarantees financial autonomy to the PRIs. Specific responsibilities have been entrusted to the Panchayats to prepare plans for social justice and economic development in respect of matters listed in the Eleventh Schedule of the Indian Constitution. Thus, enough care has been taken to make the Gram Panchayat an effective institution of grassroot democracy ensuring genuine participatory development process at the village level. The act further aims at reducing political and bureaucratic interference in rural development programmes.

Though the new Panchayati Raj Institutions have now got constitutional legitimacy, there are some pre-conditions/prerequisites, necessary for the success of the PRIs in order to fulfil the aspirations of the rural poor masses. The structural shortcomings of the Constitutional (Seventy Third) Amendment Act, 1992 and the existing socio-economic power structure in the rural areas and the country as a whole which may effect the successful functioning of the PRIs and the people's aspirations adversely.

1. The 73rd Act gives more powers to the state legislature to decide every thing such as structures, their powers/functions, very little real powers in each subject area due to poor delegation which is against the objectives of decentralisation of power. As a result, to make Panchayat institutions of self-government has been ignored in many recent state legislations. Briefly, the success of the PRIs depends on the intention of the state government as to whether they want PRIs to succeed. Even after constitutional recognition to the PRIs, the success of the PRIs largely depends on the political will of the State Government.
2. Governor is empowered to appoint Finance Commission bypassing the two layers—Panchayat Samiti and Zila parishad. In these two structures, financial matters should be discussed.
3. The very concept of decentralisation based on the donated funds from the governemnt (centre/state) is a false concept of decentralisation. Because it cultivates attitudes of patronage, corruption, irresponsibility, misuse of public money, exploitation, and nepotism. This concept neither cultivates initiative nor self-reliance. If government resources do not flow, such decentralisation would automatically collapse. The growing financial dependence of Panchayats on the Central and State Governments, has a dangerous implication. If the Panchayats do not impose taxes, it may pose a threat to their existence as a unit of self government.
4. No separate cadre for the PRIs has been provided in the Act, 1992 to ascertain accountability.

5. No inner PRIs relationship has been laid down clearly.
6. Act may encourage antagonistic relationship between the state bureaucracy and elected PR bodies, authorising the state legislature.
7. New eleventh schedule leaves out law and order. In the circumstances, calling the Panchayats a unit of self government is a misnomer. It is only an instrument to carry out development schemes.
8. Unorganised weaker section of rural society goes unrepresented despite reservation of seats. In satratified and hierarchical society of India, reservation of seats for poor general women, SCs/STs has no relevance and not possible at all.
9. Act ignores the highly exploitative power structure in our rural areas. It also ignores the reality that the poor and highly unorganised masses are in no position to use their votes for their own benefits, giving them powers without doing anything about exploitative structure is surely going to be futile exercise.

Preconditions/Prerequisites for PRIs Success Recommended

1. The elected representatives of the Panchayats should exercise superintendence and control over government officials, *i.e.* serving the Panchayats instead of playing a subordinate role.
2. The power of dissolution as well as accountability of lower level Panchayat units rest with the next higher levels of Panchayats and not with government officials in order to establish peer group accountability.
3. An effort to revitalise PRIs, in fact, is an attempt to reconstruct Indian polity by way of bringing so far deprived sections to their active participation at all levels of Panchayats.
4. PRIs should be treated as the single agency for development of the rural local levels.
5. Panchayats cannot develop as genuine units of self governance without corresponding drastic reduction and restructuring of powers and administrative set-up of the central and state governments at least in respect of items included in the eleventh schedule of the Constitution. To ensure this, reduction of

functions and structural readjustment of central and state governments should be made through the constitution of national commission.

6. There should be a single ministry of Panchayats and Nagarpalikas.
7. In the preparation and implementation of plans for economic development and social justice, NGOs, and co-operatives should be functionally associated with PRIs.
8. Numerous central and state Acts, regulations, manuals, government orders going against devolution of powers and functions to Panchayats require to be identified for appropriate remedial legislative and executive action by the central and state governments. This task should be done by Law Commission or other expert body at priority basis.
9. Functions and powers should be determined by the legislature. There should not be any scope for executive fiat in this regard.
10. To become self governing institutions, there should be true decentralised planning so that district level schemes should either be sponsored by the village or intermediate or District Panchayat but not handed over to them from above. Panchayats at three levels should have reasonable percentage of funds of state plan and financial resources which should be totally united so that they can use these funds on the basis of their priorities. These together with other sectoral outlays should constitute a district plan budget. This should be shown in the state budget to be voted by the state legislature.
11. Panchayat should be constituted for every part of the country including the areas covered under the 5th and 6th schedules of the Constitution. In these areas, the basic principles of 73rd Amendment should be harmonized with the local ethos, traditions and institutions so as to have democracy with continuity. The central law contemplated in article 243m of the Constitution should be enacted early.
12. Merely constitutional amendment cannot improve the access of the poor masses in the highest level of decision-making bodies. To ensure this, it calls for efforts in other areas like developing multi level planning frame-work, including

strengthening of micro level planning processes, integration of PRIs with planning and administration.

13. To strengthen the poor so as to protect them from the exploitative behaviour of the rural rich. The power-structure that exists today in our rural areas is likely to exploit the poor with or without Panchayati Raj. If the benefits of PRIs have to flow to the poor and if the poor are to be enabled to participate in PR activities, it is necessary that their position is strengthened by various means such as :

    (a) Attacking the dependency of the poor by plugging the points of exploitation. Efficient, public distribution system, seed banks, grain banks, social security measures.
    (b) Giving right to work to the poor so as to ensure them minimum employment and income to live on. Because poverty question is a power question. It is rooted in the model of development the country has adopted and in the socio-economic structure that obtains in the country.

14. To ensure reservation of seats for women, they have to be given support services like, health care, child care, maternity benefits and right to work. Literacy is also a major step towards the emancipation of women as it means self confidence and assurance.
15. Provision of separate PRIs cadre. The PRI members should be trained in Panchayat Act and its provisions, the objectives and functions of PRIs, dynamics of rural society, growth potential of their areas and skills of planning for overall development of their respective areas.
16. Panchayats should be entrusted with policing and judicial functions/powers to maintain law and order at village levels and to settle petty cases both civil and criminal nature.
17. It is the political will of the State Government, that is the most important pre-condition for the successful functioning of the PRIs. Political will of government may be the product of the politico-ideological commitment of the party in power. Any amount of legal reform will not bear any fruit unless there is

political will to achieve them. For example, working even within the old Act, PRIs in West Bengal have achieved a measure of success, whereas in most of the states they have failed.

18. Constitutional sanction is not an end in itself. It is not the antidote to the ills that the system of PRIs in the country is suffering from. What is absolutely necessary is a basic change in the socio-economic environment of the Panchayats through land reforms and restructuring of centre–state relations to make the state governments more powerful. A healthy State Government can give birth to a healthy local government. It is needed that devolution of power from the centre to states, states to districts and districts to Panchayat units.
19. The act provides reservation for women, scheduled castes/ scheduled tribes and backward classes to ensure their fuller participation in politics and decision-making at all levels of the PRIs. Merely providing reservation for women and weaker sections will not usher in an effective participatory grassroot democracy. The fact is that economic empowerment is an essential precursor of political empowerment. So, an effective measure to empower the weaker-sections and women economically and educationally for their meaningful participation in rural local self government should be taken. This can be only possible by bringing about genuine and effective land reforms all over the country. After all, in India, a country of villages, land is the most dominant factor/aspect in the rural power structure. If the land is redistributed to them, they would be better placed to play a meaningful role in rural affairs through Panchayats. It is thus true that effective land reforms hold the passport to a successful Panchayati Raj System under the Constitution (Seventy Third) Amendment act, 1992.
20. For implementing rural development schemes/programmes, the Panchayats should be prevented from using contractors as is practised in West Bengal. They must involve the local people directly with technical assistance by the staff and voluntary supervision by the Panchayat representatives.
21. What is needed is a consensual and uniform approach of

21. What is needed is a consensual and uniform approach of regular auditing of all expenditures incurred by the Panchayats. It is also insisted that the accounts should be shown in a public place. Besides this display of the written accounts, verbal direct communication to the common people in an open meeting is also considered essential. These are the ultimate democratic checks on the entire system.

One may hope that the 73rd Constitutional Amendment Act gives political and economic powers to the grassroot level ensuring to protect the interest of the weaker sections of the society. There is no doubt in it but for making it meaningful, socio- politico-economic power structure and property relations, generating large scale disparities in the Indian society have to be radically restructured, otherwise the weaker/deprived sections will not only be deprived of the development programmes but in most of the cases, they will be kept out of development process. As the fact remains true, the benefits of the planned development in the existing socio-politico-economic power structure cannot percolate to the weaker and neglected/deprived sections of the society.

6

OUR GOALS FOR TWENTY-FIRST CENTURY (a) Economic, (b) Social and (c) Administrative : Some Suggestions

A social scientist holds the position of an observer–analyst, and does not sit in judgment.

Goals are several. But goals are finalised on the basis of priority/ basic needs of the state by the political structure which must be acceptable to the sovereign people of the liberal democratic state, failing which, the decision in finalising the future goals of economic, social, political and administrative nature becomes contrary to the essence of popular sovereignty. Because, the people's ideas/views and visions of the future are reflected in the goals. It is also necessary to keep in mind that civil society is changing. So, goals are not static but dynamic/changing. So our goals for twenty first century have to be determined keeping in view the New Economic Policies liberalisation, privatisation, globalisation, market friendly economy and GATT Agreement affecting the socio-economic conditions of the people especially the poor/weaker sections adversely, whether we can afford to have short-sightedness or far sightedness in goal-setting and goal achievement. Because the 21st century is to cover three or four generations of youthful and working population, and weaker/deprived/disadvantaged sections of the Indian society. The expectations of the people are also rising owing to the fast changing socio-economic situations in this country and the world as well. In such situation, goals set by succeeding generations of population may lose continuity. Therefore, the framework of goal-setting must have a time dimension. So an objective oriented vision has to be required. Where there is people-centred vision, people flourish creating an alternative world order based on economic justice, environmental sustainability and political inclusiveness.

Goals of the democratic constitutional and welfare state of India such as economic, political, social, and administrative have already been enshrined in the preamble to the Constitution of India and its chapters on Fundamental Rights and Directive Principles of State Policy and other welfare measures and directives of the Government of India issued from time to time.

To translate these constitutional objectives/goals into practice for the greatest good of the greatest number, the Constitution has provided for a set-up of liberal democratic Parliamentary Government/Structure having three administrative organs, *viz.* legislature, executive and judiciary, investing popular sovereignty with the people.

Besides, Nehru-Indira Gandhi model of development/nation-building was based on relatively self reliant economic development of the country and the active and positive role of the state in the all round transformation of India.

As is experienced, the translation of these constitutional welfare goals into practice have in fact, remained a mere constitutional obligation and been far off even after 50 years of Independence, within the existing socio-economic power structure based on the capitalist path of modernisation and the market economy framework which the democratic and constitutional state of India has adopted in post-independent India. It has widened/sharpened disparities, frustration, estrangement, deprivation, exploitation, poverty, insecurity, oppression, unemployment, threats of starvation, corruption, and injustices of all sorts, affecting adversely the social, political and economic conditions of the disadvantaged, vulnerable, weaker sections and the poor women of the Indian society.

The weaker/deprived sections are not only deprived of the development programmes but in most of the cases, they are kept out of development process. Because poverty question is a power question. It is rooted in the model of development, the country has adopted, and the socio-economic power structure that obtains in the country.

The Nehru model of economic development of India was based on relative self reliance, import substitution, industrialisation and bargaining with powerful industrial countries on terms and conditions for foreign assistance in India's economic development. The Nehru model was based on the principle of the relative autonomy of the state while dealing with other nation states. The New Economic Policy of the Narasimha Rao Government is global integration of India with advanced industrial countries. This liberalisation policy, which is a decisive break with the Nehru-Indira Gandhi phase of political leadership of the Indian state, is to faster privatisation and globalisation of the Indian economy. Privatisation and liberalisation advocate reduction of government functions or less government intervention, rolling back of the state from the sphere of production and productive investment and a significant curtailment of the level of social expenditure and market – friendly economy or marketisation of governmental functions and public services, resulting in creation of a "police state" and maximisation of profits and competition and export led-industrialization to encourage foreign investment and technology, shifting from state led development. The New Economic and Liberalisation Policies are blow to the sovereignty of the Indian people in economic affairs, did not produce genuine economic growth and the Structural Adjustment Programme (SAP) attacked conditions of life and work of the working people and poor, marginalising women in various aspects of their existence as a human being.

It is also essential to keep in mind that the Narasimha Rao government being in a minority did not receive any electoral or popular mandate for the package of new economic policies.

It is, therefore, emphasised that if the liberal democratic and constitutional political system of India is to succeed, positive efforts to remove contradictions/distortions, inherent in the political system have to be taken by the political masters with conviction and determined political will. Moreover, the system must be backed by social and economic democracy. In a nutshell, for the translation of the goals—economic, social and administrative for twenty-first century—into practice for improving the wretched socio-economic conditions of the weaker and neglected/deprived sections of the society, even the political restructuring of the present political system, re-ordering human relations in the economic spheres and reversion of the New Economic Policies have to be considered/called for.

Economic

(1) State led development and community based participative development instead of market led development is to be emphasised. Because markets are not natural friends of people; they have to be made people friendly through government interventions. Briefly, the state must not withdraw from the basic responsibilities of social welfare towards the deprived and the vulnerable and infrastructure, nor unregulated foreign investment be allowed to cause social disruption. Foreign investment in consumer sectors has to be discouraged.

(2) Democratic decentralisation should be regarded as a necessary condition of social, political and economic development by complete implementation of the provisions of the 73rd and the 74th Constitutional Amendment Acts, 1992 – developing both political and financial powers from the centre to states, states to districts and districts to local self governing institutions. Centralised activities must be reduced.

(3) Re-investigation of economic growth with equitable distribution of wealth and social justice is to be emphasised. People contribute to the growth and growth contributes to their well-being.

(4) Economic reforms should be of two kinds—market and re-distributive reforms as complementary to each other.

(5) Increase in public expenditure of right kind, reducing the wrong kind.

(6) Reducing the fiscal deficit to correct macro-economic imbalance—fiscal prudence.

(7) Development of human profile—increase of investment in infrastructural development—education/health etc. Cut-backs in public health and education and neglect of agriculture reforms resulted in large scale increase in poverty, despite better agricultural output.

(8) Emphasis on agricultural reforms of both kinds—market and redistribution.

(9) Creating more jobs to tackle both poverty and unemployment. Unemployment/poverty is an economic malady and a social course. Both degrade man, generate hatred, depress social activity and economic prosperity and constitute a great liability to social stability. Poverty is man made and not God ordained. In such context, to talk of development ignoring any reference to poverty is hypocritical.

(10) Extension or deregulation benefits to agriculture, priority to agriculture and investment in rural infrastructures—irrigation, flood control, environment, social services, railways, roads and bridges, encouraging agro-based small industries, processing and farm sectors, and better facilities to farmers.

(11) A national policy on water sharing and water management to save from drought and disasters.

(12) Implementation of genuine and effective land reforms and ceiling acts all over the country, and restructuring the land-lord and landless relationships. After all India is a country of villages and land is the most dominant aspect in the rural power structure. If the land is redistributed to weaker sections and women, they would be better placed to play a meaningful role in rural affairs. This also increases domestic market opportunities.

(13) Maintaining the economic policy of liberalisation aiming at maximum industrial growth rate.

(14) Greater use of modern technology and upgrade the quality of Indian industry.

(15) Export oriented and supported.

(16) Plans to get foreign investment and support domestic entrepreneurship.

(17) Giving right to work to the poor so as to ensure them minimum employment and income to live on.

(18) Co-operative way of ownership to attain twin objectives of growth and equality ought to be encouraged, as it is a potent force for transforming the existing competitive and inequitable society into an egalitarian co-operative community.

(19) Ensuring that the drive for private profit does not result in gross inequalities, besides, the state should strengthen and support civil society rather than subsidising a few groups.

(20) People centred vision and people's response to sustain development are the primary needs.

(21) State regulated market and market regulated enterprise have to be a goal.

(22) Raise revenue by progressive taxation, *i.e.* direct taxes, effectively curb black money. Income Tax Act should be amended to tax the family income rather than individual income.

(23) Cut increasing defence expenditure and reduce it through diplomatic negotiations with Pakistan and other neighbouring countries.

(24) Reduce expenditure on internal security and solve Assam, Kashmir and other internal problems through political initiatives.

(25) Reduce subsidies which benefit the big farmers and high income class people (such as fertilizers and Higher Education) and target these subsidies on poor and weaker sections.

(26) The performance of the public sectors should be improved by stopping the interference by the bureaucrats and politicians.

(27) There should be a democratisation of the International Financial Institutions especially the World Bank and IMF.

Social

(1) Genuine and effective implementation of the social welfare

provisions and secular provisions of the Constitution of India in its chapters on Fundamental Rights, the Directive Principles of State Policy and the preamble provisions to achieve social goals.

(2) The need is to have a special multi-pronged large scale programmes having three components: (i) public distribution system—making availability of essential commodities, (ii) massive employment schemes, and (iii) social security.

(3) The state has to be actively involved in the total process of production and equitable distribution and this is the only method to promote real social sector.

(4) An egalitarian educational structure, making effective provision for ensuring the right to education in the Constitution has to be made, leading to educational equality.

(5) Minimum social service like drinking water, public/health care, public housing making effective provision to ensure the right to housing for the poor, roads to marketing and rural areas, and primary school, compulsory primary education have to be provided. Higher spending on primary education, drinking water and public health care should also be a high priority.

(6) Educational, scientific temper and development help to achieve social justice. So educationists both in the fields of formal and informal education have to be encouraged to take up the task of bringing about social and economic changes by inculcating in young and old a scientific temper.

(7) Empowerment of the downtrodden/weaker sections SCs, STs and BCs has to be ensured emphasising more class representation and more political will.

(8) For true equality to become a reality for women, sharing of power on equal terms with men must be a major strategy including reservation of seats in Parliament and State Assemblies. The Government must provide supportive services such as maternity and child care facilities. Child care should be included in the Minimum Need Programme and resources should be allocated for the same. The women must be assured the availability of wider areas of job

opportunities, equal wages for equal work among males and females; removal of overt or covert barriers to entry or to upward mobility of female worker. The government should adopt appropriate policies to curb the evil trends of marginalising women/female workers. Women's empowerment has to be in terms of equal access to factors of production, to technology, to information/knowledge, to social and family resources and legal rights to property besides social, political and economic empowerment. Social justice demands that women must play an important role in the development of a nation or the society. The women constitute nearly half of the population. Therefore, active participation of women in the socio-economic and political fields is necessary for laying down the foundation of a strong nation.

(9) Security to minorities and their equal participation have to be ensured.

(10) Change in social values, social attitudes and social institutions to achieve social goals is suggested.

(11) Religious tolerance and secular outlook emphasising to have secular politicians and secular bureaucrat to manage secularism.

(12) Economic freedom–laying stress to develop material resources as well as to have constant economic growth with equity to be made possible by the state for social sectors/justice.

(13) Implementation of the management of workers in industry and their rights.

Administrative

(1) Weberian bureaucracy with its in-built impersonality, inflexibility hierarchical structure is not quite suited to the requirements of development.

(2) Transformed bureaucracy called development bureaucracy with proper training and motivation is the primary need.

(3) Organisational innovation called organisational adjustment

to make a close fit between developmental needs and organisational format is suggested.

(4) To debureaucratise, and not unbureaucratize by means of decentralisation, people's participation and placing reliance on voluntary organisations and other people's autonomous efforts is suggested.

(5) Reducing the bureaucracy by managerialism.

(6) Training the managers and in-depth professionalisation of higher public services–deep seated reforms in education system.

(7) Separation of political and administrative matters–not serving the politicians–but power to politically appointed leadership.

(8) Call for new public management paradigm–displacing administrative management paradigm.

(9) Market based Public Administration–Entrepreneurial government.

(10) Achieving economy, efficiency and effectiveness.

(11) Earning money, not simply spending, efficient use of scarce resources.

(12) Cutting down the excess flab in government.

(13) Containing fiscal deficit – reducing government expenditure from total non-plan expenditure.

(14) Catalysing all sectors – solve community problems.

(15) Not administrative reform but administrative change.

(16) Goal and result oriented administration and people's oriented approach – less of rule of law and process are the primary needs.

(17) Demand for efficient responsive, open, transparent accessible, accountable and democratic governance–ensuring the provision of Right to Information in the Constitution of India and if not, the Official Secrets Act has to be modified to provide information to public.

(18) Support to technology progress and competitiveness.

(19) Redesigning the state – Retreating state not required.

(20) Drawing new borders and forms of association between public sector and society.

(21) International dimension of National Institutional Reform, state plus civil society.

(22) Constitutional authorities, institutions and arrangements must be allowed to function.

(23) Clean and corruption free administration – need to address prevention, surveillance and prompt and deterrant prosecution of cases of corruption in civil services, especially those involving connections with unscrupulous politicians and criminals and those affecting the interests of weaker sections.

(24) Adoption of civil service code and Charter of Ethics is required.

(25) Constitution of high powered Civil Services Board in each state for processing proposals of postings, promotions and transfers of senior officials is to be undertaken/considered.

(26) Installation of Civil Services OMBUDSMAN distinct from administrative tribunals to deal with the grievances of civil servants is suggested. Besides, creation of quasi-judicial bodies in every statutory organisation to resolve the organisational conflicts is also needed.

(27) Creating effective public grievance redressal cell at all levels.

(28) Accountability of the elected representatives to the electorate and also the system of Re-call of elected representatives are to be considered.

(29) Urgent need for judicial reform for the access of the citizens to quick and inexpensive justice, and for simple and speedy procedures.

(30) Police forces in democracy should be under the control of politically elected leaders which ensure accountability of the police forces. Police intervention in social conflicts must not be permitted. Police also needs to be democratised.

(31) Adherence to constitutional goals/principles by the public servants has to be emphasised.

(32) Election laws and procedures need to be reformed. Criminals, mafias, chargesheeters and those involving in scams/corruptions (whether convicted or cases pending

against them in judicial courts for decision) should be debarred from contesting elections.

(33) Setting up of permanent/regular HUMAN RIGHTS PROTECTION COMMISSIONS at all levels.

(34) To construct a new federal balance in India, the present centralized federation may be changed into a co-operative and federal policy.

(35) People are important, not the selfish politicians. The government has to look to the latter for the survival of the former.

7

WOMEN'S PARTICIPATION IN POLITICS AND DECISION-MAKING
Problems and Prospects

Meaning of Political Participation

The process of political participation is termed as cornerstone of any democratic system, as it is only a political means through which democracy actually comes into existence, and it is only a democratic constitution which provides political rights to the men and women to actively participate in government and politics of their state. Political rights are exercised by those men and women whom the state permits to share in the legal expression and administration of its sovereign power. In popular perception, political participation means to take part in the political affairs of the state and influence the policy of the government through exercising franchise, contesting elections and getting elected as members of the elective bodies, holding public offices, giving petition, criticising the government's policies and resisting such laws and authority having demoralizing and degenerating effects on the people. In other words, political participation is regarded as the principal means by which consent is granted or withdrawn in a democracy, and rules are made accountable to the ruled. This political participation provide the citizen with "channels of direct access to the sources of authority". Therefore, healthy, free and fair political participation are regarded as the life-belt of genuine representative, serving important functions for both the citizens and the political system. It also relates to shaping and reshaping of power, authority or influence.

But only to participate in the electoral politics is a very narrow, conventional definition of politics because it leaves vast areas of socio-political endeavour where power struggle is even more of a reality than is a legislature, where two political contenders of the same ideological persuasion might be fighting, more for personal gains. Hence, the concept of power has become central to the study of politics. The political process is the shaping, dissolution and exercise of power. Robson also says, "it is with power in society that politics is primarily concerned – its nature, basis, scope and result." It centres on the struggle to gain, or to retain power, to exercise power, or influence over other, or to resist that exercise. Lasswell sums up by saying : "What men seek in their political negotiations is power."

As the National Perspective Plan for Women 1998-2000 (N.P.P), a document of the Department of Women and Child, Government of India puts it, "political participation includes an involvement in any form or organize activity that affects or seeks to affect, these power relationships". "A critique of the N.P.P. from a perspective of the women's movement "(New Delhi, 1988) says, "party politics is not the only expression of political participation. People's organisation and movements both at the grassroots level and macro levels for transformation of society and women's liberation is to be recognised." As the document further says – Women's participation in the political process is central to their struggle against oppression. All the different aspects of women's liberation depends upon their ability to express their aspirations and demands politically." It also views women not as weaker segment of the society or as passive beneficiaries of the development process but as a source of unique strength for reaching the national goal. The plan aims at economic development and integration of women into the mainstream of economy, equality and social justice for all women. Briefly, in the field of political participation, it is essential that women, particularly rural women, must be made aware of the political rights.

What is Decision-Making?

The problem of decision is the most difficult of all the problems in public administration or management. Management is impossible without the capacity and the willingness to decide. Dictionary defines the term 'decision' as "the act of determining in one's mind upon an opinion or course of action". It is choosing one alternative among several alternatives given in a particular situation. In fact, decision is a conclusion to long deliberations. Decisions have to be made and remade in the light of the ends to be achieved. Decision is not permanent in so far as they have to take cognizance of the changed situations. In decision-making, three aspects of human behaviour are involved : (i) cognition, those activities of the mind associated with knowledge, (ii) conation, the action of mind implied by such words as 'willing', 'desire', and 'aversion', and (iii) affecting the aspects of the mind identified with emotion, feeling, mood and temperament. Based on these facts, decision-making has been defined as "a conscious and human process, involving both individual and social phenomena, based upon factual and value premises, which concludes with a choice of one behavioural activity from among one or more alternatives with the intention of moving towards some state of affairs." Thus, sharing in power can be indicated either (i) by taking part in decision-making, or (ii) by holding important and administrative positions in the government or in the ruling political party.

Woman's equal participation in the decision-making process, policy-making, planning and administration is extremely important to ensure their equality while participation in the developmental process. Equality of participation means involving the women of the community in decision-making and involving them in the same proportion in decision-making as they are proposed in the community at large. The second part of the N.P.P. also lays emphasis on the increasing participation of women in decision-making process for having a respectable status in government and society. Sharing power in some form is an important element in raising up and maintaining the social and egalitarian status of a community.

For true equality to become a reality for women, the sharing of power on equal terms with men must be a major strategy. To promote their interests effectively, women must be able to enjoy their rights to take part in national and international decision-making process. Efforts are being made to narrow down the gaps between men and women in every field. Appreciable progress has been achieved in many fields but in the field of politics, still the participation of women is very low. Women are still very inadequately represented in national and international political processes dealing with peace and conflict settlement. Efforts should be intensified to overcome prejudices, stereotyped thinking denial to women of career prospects and appropriate educational possibilities and resistance by decision-makers to change that are necessary to enable equal participation of women with men in the international and diplomatic services. Though as voter, they constitute a significant number, but their representation in various political bodies and bureaucracy in disproportionate to their strength.

There are great regional disparities in respect of women as voters. In most developed regions, women enjoyed the right to vote from the early 20th century. Upto 1945, thirty five countries out of 96 had granted right to vote to women, but these were mostly developed countries. In developing regions, it took long time for women even to exercise this fundamental right. In most African states, women got the right to vote only in the sixties, seventies, and eighties. In South Africa, it was given only in 1979 and in Iraq in 1980.

The percentage of women voters has considerably increased in all the countries, but their representation in Parliament is not very high. It is surprising that in a large number of developed countries like United Kingdom (6.3%), United States (5.3%), France (6.4%), Japan (1.4%) and India (developing country) (7.5%). The highest number of Parliamentary seats are occupied in U.S.S.R. (Russia) (34.5%), followed by Norway and Rumania (34.4% each). The representation of women in Parliaments is extremely poor. In the state legislatures, in India, the figure is not very different. But there is no doubt that an all-out effort is being made to enhance the status women in India. But the status is related to the exercise of power, both political and administrative. And unless women are able to exercise this power in large number, their power in society will not change significantly. The political participation of women in India is increasing but at a slow pace. However, the involvement of women in Panchayati Raj Institutions especially at the lowest level has been increasing. Now, the constitutional provision has been made that 30 per cent of seats in the Panchayats (each level) should be reserved for women. This is a big step forward. But the studies on women's participation in Panchayati Raj Institutions have revealed that man tries to dominate the scene. In many meetings, women's presence does not require necessary and their signature or thumb impression is taken after the meeting. In many, women have no idea about the local issues or the decision taken. Their presence is more symbolic. But these difficulties can be overcome by making women more conscious of their rights and duties by different ways such as awareness camps and consciousness raising sessions.

Briefly, the status of women is directly related to the decision-making process and unless women are associated more closely with this process, the quality and justice to women cannot be achieved.

Today, the public bureaucracies are the most powerful organs in every country. They are closely involved in initiating, functioning, deciding governmental policies, identifying the problems and their solutions. The main focus of the question, to whom the bureaucracy is expected to represent, was under constant change. Until recently no effort was made to identify women as a separate group which needs representation in bureaucracy, women was always looked as an integral part of the family whose interests were supposed to be identical. But the concept, that the men can be trustees of women and represent their effectively with public bureaucracies was challenged by many. Today, it is demanded that women should have adequate representation in public bureaucracies, as men have failed to protect their interests.

But a survey of women gives a very disheartening picture, specially of the involvement of women at the higher levels. It is difficult to access the exact status of women in civil services because of differences in national systems and classification of structures and due to non-availability of authentic upto-date gender-wise information on the subject.

However, the percentage of women in higher civil services (IAS/IPS) in India has been continuing to increase at a higher pace, though the government on its part has not made any effort to provide special facilities to women any effort to provide special facilities to women to continue the initial hurdles. Form 1972 to 1992, 53 joined the IPS which is very low percentage compared to men IPS members. However, there is a positive change in the attitude of people in general and women in particular towards the police service. Although women have entered into the Central Services much before the Independence, yet the percentage remains as to be as low as 4.

Factors accounting for the Low Participation of Women in Politics and Decision-Making

1. The lower socio-economic status of women and their continuing devaluation process intensified by government policies (New Economic Policy through Structural Adjustment Programme (SAP) tend to further marginalise women leading to reduction in employment opportunities for women workers, exclusion of women workers in the productive process, reduction of wages of women and casualisation of female workers. The process of marginalisation of women workers is going to accentuate more and more in a country like India. The ruling oligarchy has no intention to adopt appropriate policies in the right direction to curb evil trend.
2. In our traditional social perception, politics is the least suitable vocation for women and should be traditionally for men only. As such, women participate to least degree than men in all political activities.
3. Household chores and child care generally considered the women's preserve, leaves little available time for outside the home concerns. Lack of social support structures, render all public pursuits beyond women's reach.
4. Party's attitudes are also responsible for this state of affairs. Generally political parties do not favour nomination of women candidates because of their ability not to mobilise substantial resources, women, access to financial resources is negligible, hardly stand a chance of getting a seat. Moreover, the women

candidate's are also not sure of their success.

5. Male chauvinist thinking dominating political parties does not encourage women to come up in the party and reach leadership positions. Although the extent of such prejudice differs from party to party depending on their ideologies. It is an all prevailing phenomenon. Besides, in the election manifestoes, political parties normally do not take women's issues, which need special representation of women. Most parties do not set aside a quota for women or provide for reservation of seats.
6. The argument that politics is dirty and corrupt and women and their organisations should steer clear of it, has also served to isolate women from political activities/concerns. This self defeating perception has only served to deprive women of opportunities to influence the course of political action in desired directions.
7. The declining moral values, the increasing use of money to achieve the political power, lumpenisation, rapid criminalisation of the society and politics, politicalisation of criminals, fear of character assassination, and muscle power reflecting the country's deepening socio-economic crisis are some of the factors which do not encourage women to take active part in politics. These evils have a great entailing impact on the condition of women in the country.
8. Social impediments, lack of awareness, access to education, the double burden of work and household responsibility and their attitudes are also the most discouraging factors for women not to participate both in politics and decision-making.
9. The women's vulnerability is heightened primarily due to increasing unemployment and exploitation. Here, exploitation may be understood as unequal wages for equal work among males and females, overt or covert barriers to entry or to upward mobility of female labour, unequal access to females to factors of production, to technology to information and to social and family resources. Legal right to property is yet another area gaining repeated articulation in the recent past.
10. While the numerical strength of women in public bureaucracies

had gradually increased, the concentration is mostly at the entry point.

11. Selection based on merit is not always gender neutral.
12. Laws relating to equal employment opportunities and reservation (in some federating Units in India 30% seats/jobs are reserved for women) are not always implemented effectively in the true spirit.
13. The Panchayati Raj System in the wake of 73rd Constitutional Amendment stipulates reservations for the most vulnerable and traditionally under-privileged sections of the women to ensure their active participation at all levels of the Panchayati Raj System. But non-implementation of meaningful/effective land reforms all over the country is the most deterrent to such participation affecting the successful Panchayati Raj System adversely.

It has to be accepted that the involvement of women in the political participation and decision-making is a necessary step for a sound democratic society. It is the core element of democracy essential for learning, legitimacy and stabilisation. By and through it, political rights, observes. Alexis de Tocoueville, descend to the lowliest citizen. No one thus can be called either happy or free without participating, and having a share in public power.

General Suggestions to increase Women's Participation in Politics and Decision-Making Powers

1. Women should be increasingly involved in the decision-making process. This involves greater participation of women in politics. The political parties have to realise that the issues pertaining to women are not the issues to be dealt with by women only. They are to be discussed and decided at the national level. The parties must ensure larger proportion of seats at least 30% to women. Reservation of seats in Parliament and Assemblies for women must be ensured. Women's issues should be included in party manifestoes.

2. The process of election should be free and fair. Electoral Reforms must be expedited to free politics from money, muscle power and criminalisation.
3. The practice of Bi-membered constituency should be adopted for electing one male female representatives for assuring equal representation to women.
4. Political slogan to carry the message of wider participation and to eliminate miscomprehensions about politics should be adopted. Besides, the best women politician/parliamentarian award should be instituted.
5. Law enforcing agencies must extend protection to women's political action rather than use force to suppress them.
6. An atmosphere conducive to the exercise of democratic rights including the right to organise and other trade union rights to freely articulate their problems and evolve their own charter of demands should be ensured.
7. The government must provide supportive services such as maternity and child care facilities and also extend financial, material and other help to voluntary agencies providing such services. Child care should be included in the Minimum Need Programme and resources should be allocated for the same.
8. Media, women's organisation, men's organisation as well as highly placed men and women should make efforts to create social and political awareness by eliminating social constraints/ impediments to enable women to utilize their full potential as resources for national development in its economic, political, and socio-cultural aspects. There is also a need to question the existing values and of women's social responsibilities so as to participate equally.
9. To change the present attitudes/values in society regarding the women's roles and rights, to one of equal participation in all social, economic and political processes in national and international developments.
10. To counter the reactionary forces emanating from certain sections of media, economic, social and political institutions, that encourage the demotion of women from productive to mere reproductive roles.

11. There should be an intensive training programmes for women workers (Rural and Urban) on a massive scale to build up their self-confidence and enable them to rise upto leadership.
12. The States must enact Panchayati Raj Act along with the lines of the 73rd Constitutional Amendment and hold regular elections. The social workers and social organisations should interact with the women members of the Panchayats and give them advice, information and training on the informal basis so that they will be able to discharge their important responsibilities properly.

The Act also aims at making the Panchayati Raj System an instrument of local self governance and community development, an agent of grass-root democratic polity, and the bulwark of a new social order or 'sarvodaya' against the existing exploitative system. Consequently, the Act provides for a constitutional status to the Panchayats. It also gives reservations for women, scheduled castes, scheduled tribes and other backward classes to ensure their active participation at all levels of the Panchayati Raj System. Merely providing reservation for weaker sections and women will not usher in an effective participatory grass-roots democracy. The fact is that economic empowerment is an essential precursor of political empowerment. So, an effective measure to empower the weaker sections and women economically for their meaningful participation in rural local self government should be taken. This can be only possible by bringing about genuine and effective land reforms all over the country. After all, in India, a country of villages, land is the most dominant factor/aspect in the rural power structure. If the land is redistributed to them, they would be better placed to play a meaningful role in rural affairs thorugh Panchayats. It is, thus, true that effective land reforms hold the passport to a successful Panchayati Raj System under the Constitution (seventy third) Amendment Act, 1992.

13. There should be women's representation in all National bodies like Planning Commission.
14. Increasing share in bureaucracy, specially at the higher levels

should be ensured. Certain categories of jobs which are compatible with familial responsibilities should be identified.

15. Coaching Centres exclusively for Women should be set up in different parts of the country.
16. National Civil Services Test for girls in order to pick up meritorious candidates and give them proper coaching should be introduced.
17. Age relaxation for women upto 5 years should be made/ assured.
18. Sabbatical Leave may be arranged for in-service women candidates to prepare for the competitive examinations.
19. Every Selection Committee must include one woman.
20. Check on sexual harassment in services should be ensured.
21. It is an imperative to take note of the fact that the current New Economic Policy resulting in climate of privatisation, maximisation of profits and competition, unemployment, exploitation, trade union rights, and many of their traditional benefits are already under attack and this policy is bound to depress women's union participation unless resisted effectively. As the NEP makes further inroads into decision-making power of the unions and working class as a whole women will be further weakened viz. Decision-making. In a nutshell, the new economic policy would have a disastrous effect on the dignity of women as a human being. Hence, a reversion of these policies is called for.
22. The women must be assured the availability of wider areas of job opportunities, equal wages for equal work among males and females, removal of overt or covert barriers to entry or to upward mobility of female worker. The Government should adopt appropriate policies in the right direction to curb the evil trends of marginalising women/female workers.
23. Women need to be empowered at the earliest. Employment has to be in terms to equal access to factors of production, to technology, to information/knowledge, to social and family resources and legal rights to property besides social, economic and political empowerment. Because social justice demands that the women must play an important role in the development

of a nation or the society. As the women constitute nearly half of the population, therefore, active participation of women in the socio-economic and political fields is necessary for laying down the foundation of a strong nation.

Concluding Remarks

Thus, it can be said that political participation is a key to democracy and to the continuous process of on-going democratisation. If Indian democracy is to survive, it has to be organisationally based on the participation of men and women, and has to uphold the values of equality and liberation from dependence. Only by generating political power, the weaker sections and women can alter the structure of community influence and thus, open up more opportunities for themselves. But to change a society steeped in physically and socially inferior, caste and religious endogamy/values require extraordinary feat and only education and economic independence can salvage the majority of Indian women. If the complete human being is to be evolved, if there is to be harmony and peace within the family and society, there must be a striving towards a fuller equilibrium between the weaker sexes—men and women. It is the awareness of one's identity that is the first step of one's development and until this is achieved, women's development can only be a dream and not a reality.

So, the state must actively intervene to protect women's right to organise and withdraw restrictive legal and administrative provision which tend to weaken their rights in practice. Any talk of increasing women's role in politics and decision-making without creating a free and democratic atmosphere as well as bringing them to productive labour is, at a well meaning and pious wish, as the two are closely interlinked. Imaginative and unorthodox methods need to be developed to bring political and administrative change.

As is experienced, the Constitution of India itself has provided for women a significant position in the soico-economic life of the nation by ensuring universal adult franchise, representation in political bodies, right to property, equal pay for equal work and right to equality. However, in practice women do not enjoy all these rights and are still struggling for them. These fundamental rights have, in fact, remained a more constitutional obligation.

Because the translation of these rights into practice seems to be far off, within the existing socio-economic structure based on the capitalist path of modernisation or the market economy framework which the country has adopted after independence. It has widened/sharpened disparities, frustration, estrangement, deprivation, poverty, insecurity, oppression, unemployment, threats of starvation, and injustices of all sort which have adversely affected the social, political and economic conditions of the weaker sections and poor women. Therefore, if the weaker sections and women are to be liberated from inequality of class, status and power oppression, frustration, deprivation, exploitation, unemployment, injustice, land alienation and dependency, the present socio-economic structure has to be radically restructured/transformed. It may be also noted that a narrow economic approach or bureaucratic approach must give place to a new enlightened and progressive policies for bringing about the basic socio-economic changes in the position and status of women and thereby enabling them to actively participate in politics and decision-making powers.

SELECT READINGS

Almond, G.A. and G.B. Powell, *Comparative Politics : A Developmental Approach*, Boston, Litle Brown, 1966.

Aleem, M.A., *Women in Bureaucracy.*

Aleem, Shamim, Political Participation and Share of Women in Political Power, (papers presented at the Annual Conference of IIPA, New Delhi, 10th Oct., 1993) unpublished.

Datta, Meera, Economic Policy and Status of Indian Women, *Mainstream*, Vol. XXXII, No. 33, 1994.

Easton, David, (2nd Ed.), *The Political System*, New York, Knop, 1971.

Goel, M.L., *Political Participation in a Developing Nation : India*, Bombay, Asia Publishing House, 1974.

George, J., Adjustment with Gender Equality, *Mainstream*, Vol. XXXI, No. 20, 1993.

——, The Indian Journal of Public Administration, *Quarterly Journal of IIPA*, New Delhi, Oct.-Dec., 1989. Vol. XXXV, No. 4.

——, Administrative Review, *Journal of IIPA*, Aizawal Local Branch, Annual Issue, 1993.

——, Political Science Review, *Quarterly Journal of Department of Political Science*, University of Rajasthan, Jaipur, Vol. 26, No. 1 - 4, Jan. - Dec. 1987 (published in June, 1989).

——, Teaching Politics, *Quarterly Journal of Political Science*, Deptt. of Political Science, University of Delhi, Vol. XIV, No. 2, 1988, Vol. XV, No. 2, 1989 and Vol. XVI, No. 4, 1990.

——, The Public Administrator, *Journal of IIPA*, Maharashtra Regional Branch, (Special Issue) 1993-94.

Haksar, Nandita, Draft Perspective Plan for Women, *Mainstream*, New Delhi, Vol. XXVI, No. 38, 1988.

Prasad, Chandra Bhan, Feminist Movement : Forgotten Caste Factor, *Mainstream*, Vol. XXVI, No. 42, 1988.

Singh, Gopal, Shyam P. Sharma and Prem R., Bhardwaj, Structural Adjustment and Female Workers, *Mainstream*, Vol. XXXII, No. 14, 1994.

——, *Mainstream*, Vol. XXXIII, No. 15, 1995.

——, *Alternative Economic Survey - 1993-94*, published by Public Interest Research Group, I.P. Extension, New Delhi.

8

NATIONAL AGENDA OF THE NEW GOVERNMENT
Administrative Dimensions–An Appraisal

The National Agenda of the Government is no more than a list of wishes or issues, which are the product of a different grouping of political parties. These issues are a reiteration of both outstanding national priorities/tasks and constitutional goals/obligations. The National Agenda does not indicate a major structural shift and institutional change in the existing socio-economic model of development on capitalist lines and social and property relations. It does not also amount to be qualitatively different policy regime in the sense that the possible translation of the NAG into practice is unlikely to mark a qualitative break of departure from the past. Not only but these policies/issues appear to be based on adhocism, tokenism and paternalism. There are no strategies/models/methods to implement them spelled out. Briefly, the NAG cannot be taken as any guide to development policy or approach to planning. However, the question arises whether these outstanding priorities/issues/wishes are feasible to be achieved within the existing capitalist model of development or market led development, socio-economic power structure, and New Economic Policy (liberalisation, privatisation and globalisation) and constraints of Weberian Bureaucracy with its in-built impersonality, inflexibility and hierarchical structure, given other institutions and available resources of finances. In reality the market led economy and governance in India is anti-democracy. The fact is that the NAG and constitutional socio-economic goals are unlikely to become reality so long as the present policy framework remains operative, as has already been experienced during the last fifty years of Independence. The benefits of the planned development in the existing socio-politico-economic power structure cannot percolate to the weaker/neglected/deprived sections of the Indian society. In other words, there cannot be any improvement in the life of the peripherised masses without institutional change, change in the distribution of assets and incomes in favour of the poor, which is not possible without genuine and determined political will. This in turn, depends on a change in the correlation of inter-class forces in favour of the deprived masses.

Despite all this, there are some suggestions appended below regarding the possible materialisation of he NAG and constitutional socio-economic goals :

1. Honest governance in the country being a capitalist oriented, class divided and an acquisitive society appears to be a distant dream. Till private property remains the symbol and status of power, the desire to acquire it by any means remains preponderant among the individuals. The desire of rich to become richer make them blind to any value pattern. It is not poverty, but the desire to be rich in a capitalist society is the root cause of the evil and dishonesty. To have an honest governance is the creation of new social order based on social ownership of property, equitable distribution, fairplay and justice (social, political, economic).
2. To ensure open, transparent, accessible, accountable and democratic governance, the provision of Right to Information, if not, the official Secrets Act has to be made and modified to provide information to the public.
3. The government without political will cannot be efficient under the New Economic Policy (liberalisation/privatisation/globalisation/WTO). Globalisation undermines the conditions of self rule, self governance and self organisation especially in the countries of the Third World. It has made the citizen disappear and it has reduced the state into being a mere instrument of global capital. It is, in this economic framework,

the political will of the government is the most important precondition for the efficient functioning.

4. National Agenda of the government emphasises the growth in national economy through Swadeshi. Swadeshi is an anti-colonial concept referring to structures of power to colonies. To the Swadeshi philosophy, people possess both materially and morally what they need to evolve and design their society and economy and free themselves of oppressive structures. Economic freedom according to Swadeshi is based on endogenously driven development rather than externally controlled development. In other words, economic freedom is more freedom for the people of India to have secure livelihoods, to have control over the policies and resources that make their livelihoods. Since the present government pursues the new economy policy (liberalisation, privatisation, globalisation, WTO, Multilateral Agreement Investment (MAI) and Structural Adjustment Programme), Swadeshi plank cannot be operative. So, the government must review its liberalising decisions and reverse the trend to side step, otherwise its solemn commitments to Swadeshi can also face mass protest.
5. Unregulated foreign investment to cause social disruption should not be allowed. Foreign direct investment in consumer, agro-processing and social sectors has to be discouraged, though the present government has permitted 100 per cent FDI in tobacco and liquor industries. Both are health hazards.
6. The Export-Import Policy (Exim Policy) is the main policy instrument for controlling exports and imports and it is generally to have impacts on domestic production, livelihoods and environment. So restrictions in the Exim Policy to an extent has to be continued, though trade liberalisation pressures require the removal of restrictions in the interests of global traders.
7. State led development and community based participative development instead of market led development have to be emphasised. The state must not withdraw from the basic responsibilities of social welfare towards the deprived and vulnerable and infrastructural development.
8. Re-invigoration of economic growth with equitable distribution

of wealth and social justice needs to be emphasised. People contribute to the growth and growth contributes to their well-being. Economic reforms should be of two kinds–market and redistributive as complementary to each other.

9. Reducing the fiscal deficit to correct macro economic imbalance—fiscal prudence. Declining tax ratio and growing negative balance of current revenue and recovery of user charges have to be checked and ensured.
10. Increase in public investment and expenditure of right kind such as infrastructural development of human profile education, health, other social sectors and agricultural reforms, reducing the wrong kind such as misused and diversion of public funds and cost and time overrun of projects. Investment in human capital formation is now considered necessary for sustained economic growth.
11. Poverty and unemployment questions are a power questions rooted in the development model, the country has adopted, and the socio-economic power structure that obtains in the country. Both have been increasing since the adoption of the New Economic Policy of the government (WTO and SAP). The eradication of the poverty and unemployment, an economic malady and a social curse constituting a great liability to social stability depends on the restructuring of the existing socio-economic order based on Western development models/ideas, human relationships and state intervention and not on the retreating state. In fact, the liberal democratic state of India is not a regulator but only a facilator. Employment is created under the government/public sector and not under the private sector. The government must ensure job guarantees. Briefly, Western development model and new package of policies have a jobless growth and cannot alleviate poverty.
12. Employment objective needs to be revised from "attaining the full employment situation" to attaining "improved work structure in terms of productivity and income". Besides, manpower planning has to be integrated with production planning.
13. Rural development in the Indian context denotes state intervention in alleviating rural poverty. Corporatisation of land

meaning depeasantisation has to be stopped. In a labour surplus agrarian economy, depeasantisation is not only an economic folly, it is a direct threat to the stability of the state.

14. An effective measure to empower the rural weaker sections and women educationally and economically for their meaningful participation should be taken. This can be only possible by bringing about genuine and effective land reforms all over the country. After all, in India, a country of villages, land is the most dominant factor/aspect in the rural power structure. If the land is redistributed to them, they would be better placed to play a meaningful role in rural affairs through Panchayats. This also increases domestic market opportunities. But all this needs a strong political will of the government to implement such socio-economic measures which may be product of the politico-ideological commitment of the party in power. However, the NAG lacks such commitment.

15. The NAG does not talk of strengthening the Panchayats to become effective instruments of participatory self-governance for rural development. The fact is that democratic decentralisation is regarded as a necessary condition of social, political and development by complete implementation of the provisions of the 73rd Constitutional Amendment Act, 1992 devolving both political and financial powers from the centre to the states, states to districts and districts to rural local self governing institutions. Faith in empowering Panchayats as the indispensable means of attaining an egalitarian economic and social order has to be affirmed. Without strengthening Panchayats, any programme of economic reform in this country is rendered a mockery. Centralised activities must be reduced.

16. The purchasing power of vast majority of the people living below the poverty line cannot be raised in the market economy. They will be kept outside the market mechanisms. Food security to all poor people, all the time cannot be ensured without ensuring full and adequate security to earn livelihoods in the normal course of their activities. The operation of the present policy framework in having a food security as an integral part of an equitable, dynamic and sustainable form of economy,

and as a component of generalised livelihood and enhanced purchasing power has to be reconsidered/modified.

17. With the adoption of New Economic Policy (liberalisation, privatisation, deregulation and globalisation) public health has become a major causality. Public health is no longer a function of the states. Private sector or market oriented strategies of health provisioning cannot provide a health care for more than 350 million poor people living below poverty line. So public health system needs a complete overhauling : The development strategy and the specific institutional means rather than a segment of development package to ensure a health care to all the poor and deprived have to be evolved. Higher spending on drinking water and public health care should also be a high priority considering the fact that health is the means of development.

18. An egalitarian educational structure, making effective provision for ensuring the right to education in the Constitution has to be made, leading to educational equality. Higher investment on education has to be made by the State. Education is both means as well as the end result of development. It is one of the basic needs of the people and their human rights. It is the most powerful instrument for the empowerment of the people.

But the New Education Policy of the Indian Government under the Structural Adjustment Programme imposed by World Bank/IMF includes science, computer, professional and management education through private institutions which contradicts constitutional provisions and the NAG education for all. Education for all especially the poor in our grossly unequal/class divided society and the existing New Education policy, appears to be a more slogan unless class relations and education policy need restructuring.

19. To provide housing for all in the existing socio-economic order and the present policy framework appears infeasible. Moreover, the retreating state of India connot translate this agenda into practice keeping in view the fiscal crisis. However, it may be possible to an extent by making effective provision

to ensure the right to housing for the poor. This also depends on the strong political will of the government.

20. The NAG talks of eliminating child labour without referring to any strategy/structure where as the Child Labour Regulation and Abolition Act, 1986 defines child as child below 14 years but does not ban child labour even in hazardous industries. This wish of the present government contradicts its own Act. If the government is really serious to give effect to its pious wish, the existing Act of 1986 needs to be repealed/modified. Secondly child labour is a result of poverty and unemployment. Poverty and unemployment questions are a power questions rooted in the Western/capitalist mode of development, that the country has adopted. India cannot afford to abolish child labour because poor children and poor parents need the child income. Since it relates to poverty and unemployment, these two have to be eradicated by the state by structural/institutional changes in the existing model and policies, otherwise it appears impossible in the market led development. To feed hungry children of around half million parents living below poverty line, educate them and give them medical care in the present policy framework seems to be unworkable or simply a wish/desire.

21. For true equality to become a reality for women of sharing of power on equal terms with men must be a major strategy including reservation of seats in Parliament and State Assemblies. The government must provide supportive services such as health care, maternity and child care facilities. Child care should be included in the Minimum Need Programme and resources should be allocated for the same. The women must be assured the availability of wider areas of job opportunities equal wages for equal work among males and females, removal of overt or covert barriers to entry or to upward mobility of female worker. Besides, women's empowerment has to be in terms of equal access to factors of production, to technology, to information, to education, knowledge/training/skill, to social and family resources and legal rights to property. Literacy is also major step towards the

emancipation of women as it means self confidence and assurance.

22. The NAG commits to ensure safety and security of all citizens of all part of the country and also effective steps to make Indian free from riot and terrorism without spelling out strategies and methods. The governments at the centre and state have been expending a lot of money/resources on the maintenance of police and para military forces. Despite, the movements and riots of all sorts like insurgency, terrorism, agrarian social conflicts, internal disturbances and communal divide still continue to be turn by strifes. The genesis of these movements is mainly deprivation, economic backwardness, regional economic imbalance and neglect, unemployment. These movements breakout only for soico-economic redressal. Briefly, a wide spread violence or serious and costly disorder riot or insurgency is an expression of the failure of the nation-building. But Indian liberal democratic state has not learnt any lesson from the failure of the police to contain social, political and economic conflicts. The central and state governments have not made a distinction between the causes and symptoms of social unrest. While police can deal with the symptoms – a riot, it is beyond its power to root out the causes that spark it off. In short, the police can intervene to maintain law and order but it neither resolves the basic contentious issues nor be substituted for government policies to resolve fundamental social conflicts. For example, agrarian conflicts are product of landlord and land relationships. So agrarian conflicts have to be resolved by attacking the root cause of rural poverty and unemployment and by restructuring the landlord and landless relationships. Communal divide cannot be responded by the police. It has to be politically responded by cementing majority and minority relationships. Besides, the development strategy has to be concerned with all the different dimensions of social relationships in the country.

23. The National Agenda of the government ensures to establish secular society based on civilized, humane and just civil order without giving any reference to the existing social structure

and class character of the state power in India. The capitalist state of India based on class, caste and religious divisions cannot have secular society/a spirit of fraternity of the vulnerable and the very poor sections of Indian society liberty, equality and dignity. Briefly, a multi-religious society cannot have democratic and federal state without secularism. Secularism cannot be possible, if secular politicians and bureaucrats are not managing it. It is only democracy based on secularism which will keep India united and the other road will lead to violence and disintegration of the country. So re-ordering human relations in the economic sphere between the rich and the poor to eliminate the exploitation of the disadvantaged/deprived sections of the society has to be made. Besides, to construct a new federal balance in India, the present centralised federation may be changed into a co-operative and federal polity.

24. Discouraging maximum external dependence and indiscriminately adoption of capital intensive western technology and adopting/encouraging strategies based on the country resources.
25. Raise revenue by progressive taxation, i.e. direct taxes, effectively curb black money. Income Tax Act should be amended to tax the family income rather than individual income.
26. Reduce subsidies which benefit the big farmers and high income class people (such as fertilizers and higher education) and target these subsidies on poor and weaker sections. Contain fiscal deficit by reducing government expenditure from total non-plan expenditure.
27. The need is to have a special multi-pronged large scale programmes having three components: (1) Public Distribution System – making availability of essential commodities, (2) massive employment schemes, and (3) social security.
28. Transformed bureaucracy called development/socially responsive bureaucracy with proper training and motivation is primary need. Besides, goal and result oriented administration and people/poor oriented approach – less of rule of law and process are the primary needs.

29. Creating effective public grievance redressal cell at all levels.
30. Adherence to Constitutional goals and policies by the public servants has to be emphasised.
31. Amartya Sen has also suggested that if India can spend more resources on education, health and implement land reforms, democratic strength of India can be restored.

•

Now, it is relevant to conclude that poor or low or biased performance of the state has definitely weakened the democratic legitmacy. Gunnar Myrdal in his book *Asian Drama* has characterised India as a "soft" state because of its incapacity to restructure social relations in the face of powerful social groups. Our analysis is that India is a "vulnerable" state because a large section of society feels that it has been marginalised by policies of neglect by the state.

9

INDIA'S POPULATION POLICY
Challenges Ahead and Strategies Therefor

Rapid population growth in India has led to an increasing concern among the people of different walks of life. A majority of them believe that this staggering rise is a dreadful menace to the development of the country. If the present rate of increase continues unchecked, the country's population at the turn of the century may well reach the staggering figure of one billion. The country has already reached this figure. The country thus has been facing the greatest challenge in containing and stabilizing the growing population. So a policy to ensure success in tackling this problem/challenge has to be objective basis of the country's resources, the conditions of socio-economic development, the availability of the alternatives in the given development model and technological level of the country and the people's aspirations. The formulation of such policies concerning the population planning at all levels has to be made realistic and their implementation, monitoring and evaluation have to be ensured. Briefly, population planning, not only population control should become the main thrust and commit in the overall efforts of the country's development planning; though the country has not been able to evolve a meaningful population policy and implement it.

However, a comprehensive National Population Policy was drawn up and presented to Parliament by the Ministry of Health on 16 April, 1976 but it did not become an Act. Thus, as of today, the country does not have an approved population policy. So, the urgent need for a national consensus on population policy followed by a multipronged drive and sustained multi-disciplinary efforts to spread the message of population control to all section of the society has to be emphasised.

Problems/Challenges

1. Low literacy/educational levels, poor health standards, health care, low age at marriage, unsafe motherhood, lack of the availability of spacing methods, low practice of family planning, strong son preference, reproductive rights, poverty and poor economic standards, infant and child mortality rates, malnutrition, mass diseases, inadequate family welfare services, lack of proper child and women development strategies, drinking water, sanitation, minimum housing, clothing and social/ food security to the people at large, status of women and economic development, unemployment among women and their exploitation – unequal wages for equal work among males and females, lack of empowerment of women in decision-making processes, effective land reforms and decentralisation of power leading to poor rural development, political will and sustained administrative support. The landless people have no motivation to limit their family size.
2. The non-adoption of a democratic population policy is also a major challenge.
3. The western/capitalist path of development/modernisation adopted by the country also affects the population planning adversely. The lower socio-economic status of women and their continuing devaluation process intensified by the government policies (New Economic Policy through structural Adjustment Programme) tend to further marginalise women leading to reduction in employment opportunities for women workers, exclusion of women workers in the productive forces, reduction of wages of women and casualisation of female workers. Population control, thus, goes much beyond the family welfare sector.

Strategies for Population Policy

It is clear from the above that there is an urgent need for definite population policy and action programmes to control the rapid population growth. Some tentative strategies/measures are further considered towards in this direction.

1. Measures should be taken to accelerate reduction/decline in infant and child mortality and fertility, malnutrition and mass diseases. For achieving these objectives, a provision of good health standards, safe motherhood, family welfare services and minimum of food, cloth, shelter/housing, sanitation, drinking water and social security for all especially the poor, disadvantaged and deprived sections of the Indian populace/ society has to be made by the constitutional liberal democratic state of India.
2. Provision of primary education for all especially the girl child, greater economic equity and social justice, state led development, social participation in development or community based participative development and better and more easily accessible family planning services has to be emphasised/ ensured.
3. For achieving rapid decline in unwanted fertility and population stabilisation, the government must provide supportive services to women particularly poor and weaker females/workers such as health care, maternity and child care facilities. Child care should be included in the Minimum Need Programme and resources should be allocated for the same.
4. The women must be assured the availability of wider areas of job opportunities especially outside home, equal wages for equal work among males and females, removal of overt or covert barriers to entry or to upward mobility of female workers.
5. Women's empowerment has to be in terms of equal access to factors of production, to technology, to information, to education, knowledge/training/skill, to social and family resources, legal rights to property, to independent income, and to proper representation in managerial, political and

administrative positions of power and responsibility/decision-making processes. For true equality to become a reality for women of sharing of power on equal terms must be a major strategy. Literacy is also major step towards the emancipation of women, as it means self confidence and assurance.

6. Panchayati Raj Institutions and other forms of local self government are better suited to implement population stabilisation programmes. With this in view, there must be effective democratic decentralisation of administration with devolution of both political and financial powers from the centre to state, states to districts, and districts to both rural and urban local self governing institutions to carry out and supervise social, political and development programmes including population stabilisation programme such as family planning, primary education and primary health care. Faith in empowering Panchayats as the indispensable means of attaining an egalitarian economic and social order has to be affirmed. Without strengthening panchayats, any programme of economic reform and population stabilisation programmes in this country is rendered a mockery. Centralised activities must be reduced.
7. Economic empowerment is an essential precursor of political development. So weaker sections and women have to be empowered economically and educationally, for their meaningful participation in rural local self government should be taken. This can be only possible by bringing about genuine and effective land reforms all over the country. After all, land is the most dominant factor in the rural power structure. If the land is redistributed to the poor and landless rural masses, they would be better placed to play a meaningful role in rural affairs and population stabilisation programmes. This also increases domestic market opportunities. But all this needs a strong political will of the government to implement such socio-economic measures which may be the product of the politico-ideological commitment of the party in power.
8. A democratic population strategy calls for huge investment in human profile education, public health care and other social

welfare sectors, as the bulk of Indian population is extremely poor and is already heavily taxed by indirect taxation methods. Is the Indian state prepared for all this? But with the adoption of New Economic Policy (liberalisation, privatisation, globalisation and deregulation) public health has become a major casuality. Private sector or market oriented strategies of health provisioning cannot provide a health care for poor men and women living below poverty line. So public health system needs overhauling. The development strategy and the specific institutional means rather than a segment of development package to ensure a health care to all the poor and deprived sections have to be evolved. Higher spending on drinking water and public health care should be a high priority considering the fact that health is the means of development.

9. An egalitarian educational structure/educational equality to ensure the right to education in the Constitution has to be made. Higher investment on education has to be made by the state. Education is both means as well as the end result of development. It is one of the basic needs of the people and their human rights. It is the most powerful instrument for the empowerment of men and women. It also helps population stabilisation programmes. But education for all especially the poor men and women in our grossly unequal/class divided society and the existing New Education Policy appears to be infeasible unless class relations and education policy need restructuring.

10. Eradication of poverty and unemployment has to be done/ ensured for population stabilisation/control. But it is not easy in the existing capitalist socio-economic order. Because, poverty and unemployment are a power questions, rooted in the development model, the country has adopted and the socio-economic power structure obtains in the country. Both have been increasing since the adoption of the New Economic Policy of the liberal democratic state of India (liberalisation, privatisation, globalisation, deregulation, WTO and SAP). The eradication of poverty and unemployment depends on

restructuring of the existing socio-economic order based on western/capitalist model, human relationships, state intervention and not on the retreating state. Poverty and unemployment are eradicated by the state and not by the market/private sector. Briefly, western capitalist development models have a jobless growth and cannot alleviate poverty and the problems of unemployment, malnutrition, mass diseases, infant and child mortality cannot be tackled.

However, it is further suggested that employment objective needs to be revised from "attaining the full employment situation" to attaining "improved work structure in terms of productivity and income". Besides, manpower planning has to be integrated with production planning.

11. Property relations will have to be restructured as a prerequisite for the success of any development effort. Restructuring of property relations in land and industry needs to be done simultaneously. As the fact is true, the benefits of the planned development in the existing socio-politico-economic power structure cannot percolate to the weaker and neglected/deprived sections of the Indian society. So reordering human relations in the economic sphere between the rich and the poor to eliminate the poor men and women's exploitation has to be made.
12. Due recognition should be. given to human beings as producers of material values and not only simply consumers.
13. Population stabilisation programmes cannot be possible under the New Economic Policy (liberalisation, privatisation, globalisation/ W.T.O). Globalisation undermines the conditions of self-rule, self governance and self-organisation. It has made the citizen disappear and it has reduced the state into being a mere instrument of global capital. It is in this economic framework, the political will of the government is the most important pre-condition for the success of population stabilisation policies/ programmes. But there is a point to be noted that the political will of the government may be the product of the politico-ideological commitment of the party in power. Any amount of

legal reforms and policy formulations relating to population stabilisation/control will not bear any fruit, unless there is political will to achieve them.

It is relevant to conclude, noting that the family welfare/ development sector depends on the social welfare/development sector. If the liberal democratic state of India really wishes to formulate population stabilisation policies/programmes, social developments along with institutional change and change in the distribution of assets and income in favour of the poor have to be undertaken keeping in view that development is not the proper and all inclusive concept to describe human progress. What is indeed at stake today is not development as such, but the quality of life which goes far beyond immediate materialism, per capita income and mechanised HDI and HFI (Human Freedom Index). In brief, development strategy has to be concerned with all the different dimensions of social relationships in the country.

It may be further noted that Amartya Sen has correctly suggested that if India can spend more resources on education, health and implement land reforms, democratic strength of India can be restored. This, in turn, can help formulating the democratic population development strategy, as regards the population stabilisation policies/programmes.

10

CONFLICTS OF PLURAL SOCIETY AND THEIR IMPACT ON INTERNAL SECURITY

Modern Dynamic Plural Society according to Robert Dahl inhibits the concentration of power in any single unified set of actors. It disperses power among a number of relatively independent actors. Because of their power and autonomy, the actors can resist unilateral domination, compete with one another for advantage, engage in conflict and bargaining, and pursue independent actions of their own. Characteristic of modern dynamic plural society is a dispersion of political resources such as money, knowledge, status, and access to organisations of strategic locations, particularly in economic, scientific, educational and cultural affairs; and of bargaining positions, both overt and latent in economic affairs, science, communications, education and elsewhere.[1] As regards the pluralist characteristics, Indian society is neither modern nor dynamic. A typical Western Modern Dynamic Pluralist society, as visualised by Dahl is neither possible nor probable in the Indian context on account of the historical and economic limitations imposed by colonialism and the feudal agrarian background.

So far as India is concerned, India is a classic and most complex Plural society and a federal polity. India's Plural-Federal character is apparent in practically every major aspect of its collective life; be it social systems; economic formations; culture-patterns or language-dialect grouping; religious communities; castes; sub-castes, and sects or local variations of commonly prevalent methodologies, and commonly revered deitieds, or ethnic identities; regional alignments, and sub-regional attachments, or diversities of history marked by moments of triumphs; and tragedies and differences in heroes, and villains; and in the rich tapestry of folklore, folk dance, music, cuisine, crafts and artecrafts of life.[2]

Indian federalism is thus composed of segments constituting language and dialect groups, religious communities, denominational sects, castes and sub-castes, regional and sub-regional configurations, ethnic formations and defined cultural patterns.

There was two dichotomies in India's federal polity–the social dichotomy manifested horizontally in the existence of multi-regional identities subsuming varied *jatis*, religious and language communities and culture patterns, and the economic dichotomy manifested vertically/hierarchically in each region in terms of caste, class and income group. To overcome both the dichotomies for a better national integration, commitment to the generic process of equality with human rights and individual liberties has been recognised by the framers of the Constitution as a basic pre-requisite of national reconstruction. It is in this normative framework that the twin strategies of secularism to overcome the horizontal cleavage, and social justice (implied in the slogan of socialism), to overcome the vertical cleavage have been sought to be simultaneously operationalized within the framework of a participatory democracy.[3]

There are also some characteristics of the plural-federal society of India to be noted :

(i) Since unity in India is itself a federal concept, it follows that it is unity born out of the interdependence of diverse segments covering 15 distinct languages in over 350 dialects, and scores of dialect groups 8 major religious communities, thousands of *jaties*, 60 regional and sub-regional configurations and defined cultural patterns, all competing and co-operating in the building of a unified civilization.

(ii) Religious communities in India reveal an asymmetrical pattern in which there are two gigantic *viz.:* Hindu and Muslim, two significant *viz.:* Christian and Sikh and the rest miniscule segments.

(iii) The term minority is a quantitative term that emphasises numbers and overlooks the essence of a human situation; it is therefore better to perceive India's plural society in terms of socio-cultural segments and that too at the different regional levels, rather than in a unilinear scale of one majority and the rest as minorities in an all India context.

(iv) Only Hindus and Muslims constitute large all India segments while all other religious communities are either a multi-regional or only sub-regional dimension, and much against common impression, the bulk of the Muslims like the caste Hindus and Harijans live in rural hinterland.

(v) Because of their size and spread, what is called the Hindu problem and Muslim problem, is essentially the problem of India, a national problem and not a communal problem or the problem of a community, because Hindu and Muslims are the only two all India communities who are composed in several distinct sub-communities–regionally, linguistically and ethnically.

(vi) Since India is the second most populous country in the world, particularly every major national problem becomes at one level, the problem of numbers, and further since India is an ancient and continuing civilization, therefore, most problems also acquire a depth and complexity of history.

Liberal Democratic Constitution of India and Pluralist Values/ Provisions

(1) The democratic Constitution of India enshrines pluralist values. It incorporates the provisions of the preamble such as Sovereign, Socialist, Secular, Liberty, Equality and Fraternity for the democratic and just governance of the Indian masses irrespective of any discrimination based on caste, communities, sex, creed, religion, region, language, ethnicity and the rich and the poor.

(2) It guarantees Fundamental Rights, only political as well as civil, religious as well as socio-cultural to one and all. But these rights neither give economic rights to the Indian masses, nor emphasise mass action and participation resulting in common good and equality.

(3) The liberal democratic Constitution of India has some Directive Principles for the state to strive to promote a social order through the instrument of 'Political democracy' in which justice-social, political and economic shall inform all the institutions of nation life, assuring the dignity of the individuals and unity of the nation. These directives are not justiciable but it shall be the duty of the state to apply these principles in making laws for the greatest good of the greatest number.

(4) Democratic system also permits and even prompts and promotes people's right of dissent, of articulation, of demands, of formulating and projecting alternative solutions to common problems.

(5) India's federal polity based on adult universal franchise, representative institutions, responsible government, rule of law and independence of judiciary supported by a vigilant media, and active organs of public opinion is bound to allow and even encourage the crystallisation of interest orientation and interest articulation of its many segments—linguistic, religious, ethnic, regional, cultural, professional and politico-ideological. This is part of democratic bargaining, part of political culture of an open society given to accommodation and reconciliation of varied demands.

(6) Establishment of an egalitarian society which entails equity and justice for sections of the society without any discrimination. Certain castes (SCs/STs/OBCs) in India are socially and educationally backward and economically weaker. Therefore, they have been given special privileges by the Indian Constitution and law to bring them at par with the rest of society.

(7) The Constitution enjoines upon the state the removal of untouchability, universalization of education and planned economic development to establish a socio-economic system in which the living standards of the people improve so that equality before law and equality of opportunity guaranteed by the Constitution may be achieved.

(8) Pluralist society in India demands that all citizens, irrespective of their caste, creed, class, religion, ethnicity and sex shall enjoy

> not only equal rights but also security of life and property and avenues to promote their religion, language and culture while enjoying the fruits of economic development in an equitable manner. Briefly, the pluralist society also needs justice of all sorts—social, economic and political based on equality as an integral to most contemporary theories of justice. Justice (social/ economic) involves distributive justice or redistributive justice, i.e., distribution of resources, benefits and burdens in society according to needs, worth, merit and work. There are, thus, provisions in the Chapters III and IV on the Fundamental Rights and the Directive Principles of State Policy of the Indian Constitution to achieve justice.

The Constitution of India does guarentee all this but there are serious and complex problems as far as their implementation is concerned. Our ideals are all right, our practices are not. The distinction between the constitutional ideals and operational goals is thus, paradoxical. It may be further mentioned that the constitutional socio-economic goals have not been made into practice owing to mainly the existing socio-economic model of development on capitalist/market economy lines and social and property relations. These are unlikely to become reality so long as the policy framework remains operative, as has already been experienced during the last fifty years of Independence. Besides, the other possible bottlenecks also include the absence of decentralised political institutions, the administrative and organisational networks for reaching the geographically dispersed population of the poor, and finally, devising appropriate institutional forms as well as technologies to raise in a sustained fashion the economic viability of the poor.

Conflicts and their Impact on Internal Security

In the liberal view of political system, "Conflict" exists in terms of problems which need to be solved. Conflict does not, or need not run very deep; that it can be managed by the exercise of reason, good will, and a readiness to compromise and agree. On this view, politics is not civil war conducted by other means but a constant process of bargaining and accommodation, on the basis of accepted procedures, and between parties who decide as a preliminary that they want to live together more or less harmoniously. This sort of conflict is not injurious to society but it has positive advantages. It is not only civilized, but also civilizing. It is not only a means of resolving problems in a peaceful way, but also of producing new ideas, ensuring progress, achieving over greater harmony. Conflict is functional, a stabilizing rather than a disruptive forces.[4]

The Marxist approach to conflict is very different. It is not a matter of problems to be solved but of a state of domination and subjection to be ended by a total transformation of the conditions which give rise to it. Conflict, no doubt, may be attenuated, but only because the ruling class is able by one means or another—coercion, concessions, or persuasion to prevent the subordinate classes from seeking emancipation. Ultimately, stability is not a matter of reason but a force. The antagonists are irreconcilable and the notion of genuine harmony is a deception or delusion, at least in relation to class societies. Briefly, contradictions inherent in the structures are the primary cause for conflicts and collective behaviour manifestations in the form of direct action, strike and even riots.[5] Briefly, contradiction and conflict are often generated in the liberal political system having classes and based on capitalist model of development.

The liberal democratic and Constitutional State of India has failed to translate the pluralist values and socio-economic justice into practice for the socio-economic uplift of the socio-cultural segments and of socially and educationally backward classes of the Indian society to an extent and also to fulfil their various demands which generate tensions, often followed by conflicts and violence. Not only this but the democratic state has used excessive repression/suppression to deal with social, political and economic demands of various groups. In society which contradicts the pluralist, federal provisions such as socialist, secular, liberty, equality, and fraternity enshrined in the Constitution, educational, cooperative, social, cultural and even judicial institutions have almost lost their sanctity, credibility and sense of purpose. Social and economic disparities have widen and in the fair name of democracy, caste and anti-secular forces have been further fortified.

Besides, ever greater democratic awareness, intensification of the democratic process, ever increasing consciousness of various sections of the population of their democratic rights engenders conflict between these sections. Democracy has brought about radical change in the past power equations. The old power elites mostly drawn from the upper castes/upper strata soon find themselves being replaced by new power elites drawn from the subaltern castes and classes. Also the All India elites find themselves being challenged by the newly emerging regional elites. The changing power equations with the deepening of democratic processes thus generate intense conflict between upper castes and lower castes, between minorities and majorities, and between all-India and regional elites. These elites then increasingly use religion, caste or regional identities for mobilising support. Thus religious, caste, and regional identities acquire new significance. National identity becomes more and more secondary in the process. The pluralist model of nation-building thus comes under strain and the social space between religious, caste and ethnic groups begin to shrink. Thus, our pluralism and respect for others start to crumble :

(1) Caste war and caste-prompted conflict/violence, conflict/ struggle within castes and communities, inter-caste struggle. This has been mostly evident in Bihar, Southern U.P., Northern Madhya Pradesh, Rajasthan and Tamil Nadu, Maharashtra. At the end of 1960, 45 *Dalits* were burnt alive in Tamil Nadu. In Bihar on July 11,1996, 19 agrarian families belonging to the *Dalits* and the lower rungs of Muslim communities were butchered in broad day light by the out lawed Ranvir Sena, of the landowning classes of the Rajputs and Bhumihars. In Karnataka 8 *Dalits* (SCs) have been burnt alive in March, 2000 by the upper castes.

(2) *Internal Communal Riots/Conflicts*

Major communal riots took place—Jabalpur in 1962, Madhya Pradesh (Rourkela), Bihar (Jamshedpur) Bengal and Orissa in 1964, Ranchi in 1967, Ahmedabad in 1969, Bhivandi-Jalgaon in 1970 and Jamshedpur, Benaras and Aligarh in 1978, Moradabad in 1980, Bihar Shrif in 1981, Meerut in 1982, Baroda in 1982, Nelli in 1983, anti-Sikh (Delhi) in 1984, Bombay-Bhivandi in 1984, Ahmedabad in 1985-86, Meerut, 1987, Bhagalpur in 1989 or a series of riots in 1990 and Bombay, Surat, Ahmedabad, Delhi and Kanpur in 1992-93. They were truly savage in character and totally destructive of the pluralist values. Thousands of citizens particularly those belonging to the minority communities perished in these riots. Since late 1983, the most dismal scene prevailed in Punjab which had taken an ugly turn, with practically daily killings and reprisals, which later became a continuing encounter not between communities but between the communally minded separatist terrorists and the police. Briefly, India witnesses militant religious assertions of a section of Hindus, Muslims and Sikhs.

(3) *Inter-ethnic Conflict/Violence*

Ethnic conflicts are a product of social and political pressures and mobilisation by its leaders through the select use of ethnic symbols and politico-economic purposes. There have been a frequent ethnic conflicts in many federating units of India– Punjab, Kashmir, Assam, Arunachal Pradesh (the ruling party supports struggle to throw out the Chakmas and Hajongs from the State), Meghalaya, Nagaland – (Nagas-Kukis), Manipur (Kukis), Paites (Hmars), Tripura (Tribals and Non-Tribals) and Mizoram (Riangs and Mizos, Chakmas-Mizos). The dominant groups murder/kill the minorities to retain their domination over the areas. As a result, hundreds of lives are being lost even now. Despite the democratic polity, intolerance spreads, and the space for dialogue shrinks. Majoritarian attitude and hegemonic values are an antidote to democracy and the pluralist model of nation-building. Ethnic fundamentalism is harmful for a pluralist model.

(4) The Hindi belt constitutes the core nationality assuming a dominant role. Communal/caste politics has its strongest roots in this region. The domination by this core nationality has been

resented by the peripheral ones. This core nationality has marginalised the other nationalities. Their ethos become the dominant nationalist ethos and their culture is projected as the 'mainstream culture' but it may be also noted that a majoritarian ethos as the dominant national ethos and the dominant culture as the mainstream culture is not at all acceptable to the pluralist model of nation-building. The word 'Dominant' smacks of an anti-pluralistic spirit. What is most essential for a democratic-pluralist model of nation-building is harmonious co-existence of all religions, cultures and ethnicities without any one acquiring a dominant position. The majority community, be it religious, political, economic, linguistic or ethnic is always tempted to adopt a majoritarian approach in politics and that is what is at the root of the problem. Religious fundamentalism is also harmful to the building of the pluralist society.

(5) *Conflicts/Violence by Terrorist Gangs*

Started since 1983-84 in Punjab, since 1989 in Kashmir aided and abetted by extra-territorial encouragement, support and training and also continuing in North-Eastern States.

(6) Conflicts/Violence by Ultra-left insurrectionary elements by the Naxalites and people's war group who operated in the sixties in West Bengal, and then became more active in the Srikakulam district of Coastal Andhra and later have become more active in other parts of Andhra, Bihar and Madhya Pradesh.

(7) Political conflicts/violence are committed for specific socio-political objective by organised gangs or by adhoc groups to influence governmental decision to ventilate deep seated grievances, to punish political opponents or to intimidate locality or an electoral constituency. Most tribesmen's demands of the north-eastern region such as Nagas, Mozos, Kukis, Bodos, Manipuris, Tripuries in the fifties and sixties and later have been expressed eventually through violence. The Bombay riots on State Reorganisation in 1956, the steel plant agitation in Vishakhapatnam in Andhra Pradesh in 1966. Food riots in

Calcutta in 1958, Telangana agitation for a Separate state in 1969, Haryana struggle for a state in 1966. Save Hindi agitation in 1957, language riots in many parts of India, over the years. Shiv Sena riots in Maharashtra in 1969 and presently Bodo's movement for a separate state in Assam are varied examples of political violence/conflicts.[6]

Besides, it has been established that like in other organised activities, money-power, muscle power and brain power of the controlling groups, that give direction, are also used in riots. Enquiry reports also point out the negative role of certain politicians, police and local officials, certain types of newspapers and media, commercial elite and even some business interests in several riots.

(8) Rise of fundamentalism, communalism, parachialism, ethnic, regional identity problems, and linking religion with politics, nationality question, theory of the sons of the soil, social movements and organised form of violence supported by political parties/political masters/pressure groups, the rich and external and internal divisive/disruptive forces generate conflicts of all sorts.

(9) In the third world, democratic decentralisation has long been regarded as a necessary condition of social, political and economic development. But the democratic state of India has failed to introduce a complete decentralisation in social, political and economic spheres resulting in social vacuum that leads to social/class conflicts.

(10) No effective land reforms all over the country being the most dominant factor in the rural power structure have been undertaken except West Bengal, Tripura and Kerala, which generate agrarian unrest/conflicts and the landless poor peasants and the landlords are implicating for internal security problems.

(11) India has non-responsive rigid and frigid administration and highly proliferating bureaucracy with little accountability, non-performance of bureaucracy, criminalizing of politics—rise of goondas, mafias, mastan, speculators, black-marketeers and smugglers, unholy nexus among politicians/bureaucrats, and

criminals/industrialists and highly corrupting election system influenced by money and muscle power using castes/ communities as vote banks have threatened the unity, integrity, democratic and pluralistic processes of country.

Besides, there is a rampant corruption in public administration/public life in India. India today is among the poorest countries of the world with the largest number of illiterates and at the same time, it is considered to be one of the ten most corrupt countries of the world. It is not poverty, but the desire to be rich in a capitalist society of India that is the root cause of the evil threatening the pluralistic model and the permanent solution of the problem is the creation of new social order based on social ownership of property, equitable distribution, fair play and justice.

(12) No effective public grievance redressal cell at all levels has been set up. Disregard for Rule of Law and Human Rights by police/forces and excesses committed by police and para military forces are glaring and often reported. No permanent/ regular Human Rights Protection Commissions at all levels have been set up so far.

(13) Poor or low or biased performance of the state and uneven under-development, policies of opportunism and manipulation and adhocism in place of long term policy have definitely weakened the democratic legitimacy of the state. Gunnar Myrdal in his book *the Asian Drama* has characterised India as a "soft" state because of its incapability to restructure social relations in the face of the powerful social groups. Our analysis is that India is a "Vulnerable" state because a large sections of society feels that it has been marginalised by policies of neglect by the state.[7] All this create conflicts of different types, affecting internal security adversely.

(14) Emergence of contradictions in the political system owing to the capitalist path of development and new economic policy– liberalisation, privatisation, globalisation and market friendly economy contradicts constitutional directives and pluralist values/provisions resulting in less government. Briefly, Western model of development administration along capitalist lines and

market friendly economy emphasises economic growth, but the growth does not expand the opportunities for employment. The fruits of economic growth mostly benefit the rich leaving millions of people struggling in ever deepening poverty. The growth in the economy is not accompanied by an extension of participatory democracy of people's empowerment including gender empowerment. Material growth is achieved but people's cultural, social and ethnic identities are to wither. New economic policy leads to futureless growth meaning environment unfriendly, where present generation squanders resources needed by future generations. In short, this capitalist model of development leads to uneven and under development, a larger number of people to live below poverty line, unemployment and all sorts of conflicts/tensions, such as violent/coercive, public protests in the forms of fasts of political nature, civil disobedience movements, *gheraos* and other forms of direct action, castes and communal riots/social and political movements/violence, unrest/uprising/insurgency, terrorism, ethnic upsurge and agrarian social conflicts etc. contradicting the pluralist socialist and economic provisions of the Constitution and thereby affecting internal security adversely.[8]

Thus, structural violence is in-built in an unequal society of this country. The divided Indian society (social and economic) is itself in tension, in perpetual tussle between its affluent and impoverished parts. In this situation, the pent-up frustration and anger of the exploited/deprived have-nots leads to tension and violence. Briefly, inequality is a power relationship or relationship of domination by an individual group or class over others. These may present many kinds of differences in possessions, activities, accomplishments and so on.

Concluding Suggestions

Indian Political system with its institutions and policies has not quite been able to cope with the diverse demands of pluralist society. The system has not been able to satisfy the rising expectations of the masses. At the same time, the liberal democratic State of India has performed for better than many other countries in this respect.

In the wake of the analysis of various conflicts of plural society, the Indian political system must correct itself. Besides, some important measures to contain conflicts are required individually and collectively :

1. Although the Indian state has built up a powerful police system to deal with uprising/insurgency, communal/caste riots/tensions, social and political movements, agrarian social conflicts and other forms of internal disturbances/disorders, the country continues to be torn by strife. The genesis of these movements is deprivation, economic backwardness, regional economic imbalance, neglect and unemployment. These movements break out only for socio-economic redressal. Briefly, a wide spread violence or serious and costly disorder/riot or insurgency is an expression of the failure of the nation-building. Undeterred by the strong police presence, agrarian conflicts/unrest continue to rock rural India particularly, Bihar, Madhya Pradesh and Andhra Pradesh. The Indian liberal democratic state of India has not learnt any lesson from the failures of the police to contain social, political and economic conflicts in the country. The central and state governments have not made a distinction between the causes and symptoms of social unrest. While police can deal with the symptoms – a riot, it is beyond its power to root out the causes that spark it off. The police is active in fighting against social conflicts because the political masters and politicians without coming to terms with seminal causes of social conflicts, have abandoned their role of resolving the conflicts through political means. If this trend is not reversed, India will cease to be pluralist-federal democracy. Police can intervene to maintain law and order but it neither resolves the basic contentious issues nor be a substitute for government policies to resolve fundamental conflicts. For example, agrarian and social conflicts are product of landlord and landless relationships. So agrarian unrest has to be resolved by attacking the root causes of rural poverty and unemployment and by

restructuring the landlord and landless relationships. Communal divide cannot be responded by police. It has to be politically responded by cementing majority-minority relationships. The development strategy has to be concerned with all the different dimension of social relationships in the country.[9] The police, thus, being a part of the Indian political system often commit excesses and illegalities while ensuring law and order and dealing with the sensitive issues of communal/caste riots, social/political conflicts and ethnic conflicts/regional tensions and safeguard of Human Rights as alleged by many commissions of inquiry.

Police forces in democracy should be under full control of political elected leaders. This is the only mechanism to ensure accountability of the police forces. Police indulges in illegality, if it is not accountable to the elected representatives of the people. Police has to play a legitimate role in every society, but it has to be controlled and held leash by the law of the land.

2. Insurgency/ethnic upsurge, communal/caste conflicts/divide, religious conflicts, regional tensions and socio-politico-economic violent movements are a manifestation of a deeper malaise in the political system, socio-economic model of development on capitalist lines and social and property relations and can hardly be contained/resolved by use of army or police action. These conflicts have to be politically responded by following the strategies of accommodative pluralist and federal nationalism. A wide cross-section of the masses including genuine religious persons, women, youth, professional groups especially media persons in struggling against communalism needs to be mobilised. Groups should be sensitive to each other needs and aspirations. This sensitivity is the life-blood of a pluralist model. If one group is totally insensitive to the other's aspirations, the pluralist society will collapse like a pack of cards.

Besides, poverty and unemployment conflict questions, which are an economic malady and social curse constituting a great liability to social and political stability, are power questions rooted in the development model, the country has adopted, and the socio-economic power structures that obtains in the country. Both have been increasing since the adoption of the New Economic Policy (liberalisation, privatisation and globalisation). The Western development model and new package of policies have a jobless growth and cannot alleviate poverty. Both degrade man, generate hatred, depress social activity and economic prosperity. Poverty is man made not God ordained. In such context to talk of development ignoring any reference to poverty is hypocritical. Therefore, it may be suggested that the eradication of the poverty and unemployment and the resolution of the conflicts of all sorts depends on the restructuring of the existing socio-economic order based on the western development models/ideas, human relationships and state intervention and not on the retreating state. In fact, the liberal democratic state of India is not a regulator but only a facilator. Employment is created under the government/public sector and not under the private sector. The government ensures job guarantees. It may be further mentioned that the benefits of the planted development in the existing socio-politico-economic power structure cannot percolate to the weaker/neglected/deprived sections of the Indian society. In other words, there cannot be any improvement in the life of the peripherised masses without institutional change, change in the distribution of assets and incomes/earnings in favour of the poor which may not be possible without genuine and determined political will. This in turn depends on a change in the correlation of interclass forces in favour of the deprived/starved masses. The Indian development has been aptly summed up thus :

> "Indian experience has shown that under the existing power structure, undifferentiated approach to distribution of natural and financial resources and services secures the main benefits of distribution to affluent and privileged strata of society at the expense of the poor ones".[10]

These are the problems inherent in the Indian development strategy which defines the parameters for the possibilities and potentialities of development in all the federating units of the country.

3. State led development and community based participative development instead of market led development need to be emphasised. Because market is not the natural friend of people; it has to be made people friendly through government intervention. Briefly, the state must not withdraw from the basic responsibilities of social welfare towards the deprived, vulnerable and infrastructure, nor unregulated foreign investment be allowed to cause social disruption.[11]
4. Re-invigoration of economic growth with equitable distribution of wealth/incomes/earnings and social justice is to be emphasised. People contribute to the growth and growth contributes to their well-being. Economic reforms should be of two kinds—market and restributive is complementary to each other.
5. The major tasks for the immediate future must include: (a) restoration of the credibility of the political processes to resolve social conflicts in general and those involved in redistributive planning in particular and simultaneously, (b) to reinitiate the planned growth/process with a strong redistributive focus in a socially credible fashion. Both these tasks will have to be undertaken under the shadow of the energy constraint which may limit the options available with reference to both government and redistribution. How these formidable challenges are going to be met is a big question mark.[12]
6. An effective measure to empower the rural weaker sections and women educationally and economically for their meaningful participation should be taken. This can be only possible by bringing about genuine and effective land reforms and ceiling acts all over the country. After all, in India, a country of villages, land is the most dominant factor aspect in the rural power structure. If the land is redistributed to them, they would be better placed to play a meaningful role in rural affairs through Panchayats. This also increases domestic market opportunities. But all this need a strong political will of government to implement such socio-economic measures which may be the product of the politico-ideological commitment of the party in power.

7. Panchayats to become an effective instrument of participatory self governance for rural and urban development needs to be strengthened. Because democratic decentralisation is regarded as a necessary condition of social, political and economic development by complete implementation of the provisions of the 73rd and 74th Constitutional Amendment Acts 1992 devolving both political and financial powers from the centre to states, states to districts and districts to local self governing institutions. Faith in empowering Panchayats and Nagarpalikas as the indispensable means of attaining an egalitarian social and economic orders has to be affirmed. Without strengthening Panchayats and Nagarpalikas, and programme of economic reform in this country is rendered mockery. Centralised activities must be reduced.
8. Education, scientific temper and development help to achieve social and social justice. Education is both means as well as the end result of development. It is one of the basic needs of the people and their human rights. It is the most powerful instrument for the empowerment of the people. So higher investment on education especially the primary education has to be made by the state. Besides, educationists both in the fields of formal and informal education have to be encouraged to take up the task of bringing about social and economic changes by inculcating in young and old a scientific temper. But a mention is made here that education for all especially the poor in our grossly unequal/class divided society and the existing New Education Policy under the SAP imposed by the World Bank/IMF appears to be a mere slogan unless class relations and education policy need restructuring.
9. There is the need to have transformed bureaucracy called development/socially reponsible bureaucracy with training and motivation. Besides, goal and result oriented administration and people/poor oriented approachless of rule of law and process are the primary needs. Also adherence to constitutional goals and principles by the public servants has to be emphasised. Accountability of the elected representatives to the electorate and also the system of Recall of the elected representatives

are to be considered. Not only but the election laws and procedures need to be reformed. Criminals, mafias, chargesheeters and those involving in scams/corruptions (whether convicted or cases pending against them in judicial courts for decisions) should be debarred from contesting elections.

10. Clean and corruption free administration need to address prevention, surveillance and prompt deterrent prosecution of cases of corruption in civil service, especially those involving connections with unscrupulous politicians and criminals and those affecting the interests of the weaker sections.
11. National integration in the pluralist society of India is a very important need due to the factors as under : (i) the Indian polity is of the continental dimension and its size is large and by its diversity complex, (ii) existence for centuries of a plural society in terms of culture, language, religion, economy and urban-rural dichotomy, (iii) union type federal structure of government and administration, and (iv) democratic decentralisation involving participatory functional politics. Therefore, national integration is necessary for the modernisation of the pluralist society. It involves readjustment of loyalties of the people. The values of a tribal, a feudal and a parochial ethos give way to the ideas of a democratic, egalitarian and an evolving national society. Integration is thus movement away from traditionalist allegiances and towards a modernist allegiance – a movement for the establishment of a new national identity. Further the term 'national integration' means cohesion but not fusion, unity but not uniformity, reconciliation but not merger, accommodation but not elimination, assimilation but not extinction, synthesis but not non-existence, solidarity but not regimentation of the many segments of the people in a territorial sovereignty.[13]

Briefly, the essence of national integration is the equality of involvement and opportunity for all individuals and communities and the willingness to adopt democratic peaceful means for the attainment of all their demands. Not only that, it means security, equality, honour and involvement. It, thus, signifies conditions of unity in diversity because if there is only unity, their integration is not necessary and if there is only diversity, their integration is not possible. So, it presumes the existence of both unity and diversity. In fact, with a view to building a strong nation, cultural identities of the groups need not be eliminated. Instead of stressing on cultural distinctions, economic-inter-dependence should be fostered.

But the main challenges of India's efforts at building a new national identity by coalescing its multi-ethnic, multi-religious, multi-caste, multi-lingual, and multi-regional population around a unified national consciousness can be identified at three points : (i) inadequate distribution of goods and services, resulting in economic disparity and rampant poverty, (ii) persistence of socio-economic inequality between and within the rural and the urban segments of the people, and (iii) political populism and political exploitation by competing parties and groups by pandering to divisive, and violent communal caste and regional sentiments.[14] But the fact is that these challenges appear not to be tackled in the existing modernisation model based on the liberal democratic process and its material based captialism. All the basic premises have been changed redically since mid 1991 in the name of economic reform when the slogan has become "let the market decide." Now, the state withdraws and allows the market to play a dominant role in all economic matters. In other words, New Economic Policy emphasises a market led development instead of a state led development which accentuates polarisation between affluence and deprivation and thereby generates a narrow minded sectionalism, populist parochialism and bigoted regionalism and threats of different nature to nation-building in India. So, the western development model and new package of policies need restructuring.

12. Secularism is one of the major instruments for establishing a secular society based on civilized, humane and just civil order as well as building a modern democratic polity. It is one of the fundamental values of our national life. Secularism entails the supremacy of the democratic state—its laws, processes and

> administration over the existing pre-democratic social formation marked by loyalties around tribes, clans, sect , caste, religious and language community. It is the refutation of any form of theocratic culture and also opposed to the domination of any church, priest, or any form of organised religious authority.

The leaders and political parties generally pursue two strategies to promote secularisation of polity in our multi-religious situation. One strategy is to emphasise the unity of all religions based on their moral precepts and humanist-teachings. The second strategy to promote secularism is to emphasise the need for a civic, secular and rational ideology of political culture and state craft, and leave the question of reconciliation of religions and belief patterns to voluntary social action. True secularism can be built on the basis of genuine secular principles. The state should remain neutral, just and fair, and above either religious accommodation or religious controversy.

Major elements of secularism in the pursuit of this strategy are : (1) recognition, of religion and belief as personal and devotional aspects of life ; (2) liberation of the civic polity from religion-dominated groups and parties ; (3) enforcement of common civil laws, made and modified by elected representatives of the citizens; (4) rejection of the idea of theocratic or quasi-theocratic or religious community dominated state and the affirmation of a non-religion based democracy; (5) acceptance of scientific temper and enquiry involving rejection of dogma and the affirmation of pragma ; (6) recognition of equality of status and of opportunity for men and women irrespective of caste, colour and creed ; and (7) fraternity of the citizens as citizens and not as members of the primordial ascriptive groups—religious, linguistic or ethnic.

In Indian conditions, the elements of both the strategies for building of a secular polity need to be used. Besides, the essence of social justice as the goal of planned development means reduction in equality and removal of poverty. These two objectives are inter-related. That is, even if poverty be reduced or even removed, it need not automatically lead to reduction in equality. Both the goals would have to be pursued simultaneously and in co-ordination.[15]

There is no doubt in it but these two objectives–reduction in inequality and removal of poverty in the existing social structure and class character of the state power in India appear infeasible or to be a distant dream as these questions are power questions rooted in the development model pursued by this country. The liberal democratic and capitalist state of India based on class, caste, economic inequality and religious divisions cannot have secular society, spirit of fraternity and assure the vulnerable and the very poor sections of the Indian society of liberty, equality and dignity. Briefly, a multi-religious society cannot have a social democratic and federal state without secularism. Secularism cannot be possible, if secular politicians and bureaucrats are not managing it. It is only social democracy based on secularism which will keep India united and the other road will lead to violence, social tensions and disintegration of the country. So, re-ordering human relations in the social and economic spheres between the rich and the poor to eliminate the exploitation of the disadvantaged/deprived sections of the society has to be made. Besides, to construct a new federal balance in India, the present centralised federation may be changed into a co-operative and federal polity.[16]

With a view to contain conflicts of all sorts, positive efforts to remove contradictions inherent in the Indian political system have to be taken by the political masters with conviction and determined political will. The perspective has to be of involving the people in the control of their resources and the solution of their problems. It may be further added that with planned modernisation based on the principles of "distributive justice" and "democratic socialist arrangement", the conflicting situations will get weaker and the forces of peace and egalitarian values stronger in the long run. Besides the multiple challenges of nation-building can be met only on the basis of uniform national policies and basic struggle in India is not to deconcentrate or fragment power but to create political power which can lead the nation and defend the vulnerable strate of Indian society. To achieve this, the role of the upright, progressive and conscious citizens and the N.G.Os. is to democratise civil society by being with the people, articulating their interest and relentlessly struggling with them against national international forces of oppression. The need of the hour is goal oriented politics to build national economy, implement, national policies and create appropriate administrative, political and economic institutions for the mobilisation of the national efforts to achieve growth with equity and social justice. But all these objectives/ingredients for the pluralist and federal nation-building in the existing socio-politico-economic power structure and property relations based on the capitalist lines or the New Economic Policy (liberalisation/privatization/ globalisation) are not likely to be achieved.

So, here is a point to be noted that capitalism is a failure in development of productive forces in third world countries. This is historically a product of the uneven development. Unless social and economic structures of these countries undergo important changes, economic growth will, in fact, be reduced. So, in order to have a just and equitable social order, there is a need to have a new web of social relations, a new category of social institutions, a new devices of social control, and also a new agencies of social change such as the will to meet the needs of a rapid and harmonious development of the economic and social life of the people in consonance with the principle of equality of citizens. This is only possible through tenets of participatory socialism. Participatory socialism requires the elimination of bureaucracies and all hierarchical forms, and their replacement, not by new state or party bureaucracies, but by self-governing and self-managing people with directly chosen representatives subject to recall and replacement. Participatory socialism entails a sense of egaltarian cooperation, of solidarity of people with one another; but at the same time it respects individual and group differences and guarantees individual rights. It affords to all individuals the freedom to exercise human rights and civil liberties that are not mere abstractions but have concrete day to day meaning.[17]

REFERENCES

1. Raj, Kaleeswaram, Federal Politics and the Karala Model (in) *Mainstream*, Vol. XXXVI No. 9, February 2, 1998, New Delhi, p. 5.

2. Khan, Rasheeduddin, *Federal India – A Design for Change*, New Delhi, Vikas Publishing House, 1992, p. 8.

3. *Ibid.*, pp. 18-19.
4. Prasad, R.N., Conflicts arising out of Contradictions in Indian Political System – Their Implications for Internal Security, (Lecture delivered in the 145 Internal Security Course for Deputy Superintendent of Police and Assistant Commandant of C.P.O's. at *Internal Security Academy*, C.R.P.F. Mount Abu, Rajasthan 2-4 August, 1997, P.I. (Unpublished).
5. *Ibid.*, pp. 1-2.
6. Khan, Rasheeduddin, *op. cit.* pp. 27-28.
7. R.N. Prasad, *op. cit.*, pp. 16-18.
8. *Ibid.*, pp. 16-18.
9. Prasad, R.N., National Agenda of the New Government : Administrative Dimensions – An Appraisal (in) Administrative Review, an *Annual Journal of the Indian Institute of Public Administration*, Mizoram Regional Branch, Aizawal (1996-97 Two issues) published in 1998, pp. 103-104.
10. Kumar, B.B., (Ed.), *Modernisation in Naga Society*, New Delhi, Omsons Publications, 1993, p. 141.
11. Prasad, R.N., Our Goals for Twenty First Century : (a) Economic, (b) Social, and Administrative - Some Suggestions (in) *Review of Politics*, Vol. VI, No. 1 to 2 Jan, June and July-Dec., 1998, Deptt. of Political Science, Veer Kunwar Singh University, Ara (Bihar) pp. 22.
12. Beteille, Andre, (Ed.) *Equality and Inequality –Theory and Practice*, Delhi, Oxford University Press, 1984, p. 122.
13. Khan, Rasheeduddin, *op. cit.*, pp. 83-84.
14. *Ibid.*, pp. 79.
15. *Ibid.*, pp. 71-74.
16. Prasad, R.N., *op. cit.*, p. 104.
17. Narang, A.S., Capitalism, Development and the Third World (in) *Teaching Politics*, Vol. XV, No. 2, 1989, Journal of the Department of Political Science, University of Delhi, pp. 39-41.

11

UNIVERSITY AND POLITICAL DEVELOPMENT IN INDEPENDENT INDIA

"University stands for humanism, for tolerance, for reason, for the adventure of ideas, and for the search of truth. It stands for the onward march of the human race towards ever higher".

–Jawaharlal Nehru

Before the role of University in the political development is discussed, it is necessary to interpret the terms "University" and "Political Development" for better understanding. Indian Universities occupy today a nodal position in the effort at state-building and nation-building and social, political and economic development of the people living in the country. The Universities extend their aims beyond the responsibility of higher education to providing leadership in the social, political and economic development. The responsibility substantially rests on the Universities for promoting the acquisition of new knowledge and skills for development of physical and human resources, of transforming traditional values and attitudes to build a new society informed by equality and social justice, and of developing a climate for creative thinking and growth of individuality. It may be further mentioned that the objects of the Universities are also to disseminate and advance knowledge by providing instructional and research facilities in such branches of learning as they may deem fit; to pay special attention to the uplift of the people of the country and in particular, their intellectual, academic, socio-cultural and econo-political transformation/

advancement so that the best in the tradition is maintained and preserved while at the same time assimilating the benefits of development from the new strides in science and technology.

Political development as is generally spoken, means development from one stage to another higher stage, a process of growth over a period of time. For instance, economists may observe and measure development in terms of Gross National Product (GNP), per capita income, investments and output. For other social scientists, political development means democracy, political parties, civil, political and human rights, participation of the people in the decision-making process of the government, urbanisation, interest/pressure groups, a high level of literacy, representative government, industrial and technological advance. Political development also means the continuous emergence of stages, each of which reflects distinctive characteristics and needs. In brief, political development signifies the capacity of a political system to sustain continuous growth. Political development, in other words, involves three things : (i) development of the capability of the political system; (ii) development of the contribution of the political system to the overall development of the concerned society; and (iii) development of the responsiveness of the political system.

It may be necessary to do some fresh thinking on the meaning and purpose of political development. Development ought to mean the development not of things but of men the satisfaction of their basic needs—food, shelter, clothing, health and education. A process of growth or development that does not lead to fulfilment of these basic needs, cannot be regarded as development. Conversely, under development involves denial of basic needs to the people while enhancing the material returns to the dominant groups. It deprives the majority of their survival and sustenance. A growth process that benefits only the wealthiest minority and maintains or even increases the disparities between and within countries is not development. More correctly speaking, it is exploitation. The theory that rapid economic growth benefiting a few will 'trickle down' to the masses of the people has proved to be wrong and illusory. It has been advocated by western social scientists and gleefully accepted by the political elites in the developing countries because it suits them. The idea of growth first, justice in the distribution of benefits later has led to the growth of prosperity in the upper strata of society. In fact, it has not been followed anywhere by distribution of benefits, and has thus to be rejected. The enumeration of basic needs as mentioned above does not mean that there are not, 'other needs' 'other goals' and 'other values' which are equally important. Freedom of speech/expression and the right to gain and to receive ideas and stimulus are also regarded as equally important. One should be free to shape his own life and have a right of participation in the decisions made by the political system in the country. It may be a little further said that development includes also the right to work which means not just having a job but also finding self realisation in work and the right not be alienated through production processes that use human beings simply as tools. In other words, the essential theme of development is the elimination of poverty, social inequality and unemployment. Development is fundamentally an egalitarian goal, no doubt but the translation of this goal into practice within the existing socio-politico-economic power structure based on the capitalist model of development and the market economy frame-work, which the liberal democratic and constitutional state of India has adopted during post-Independence period, has been far off.

Keeping in view a brief understanding of the term 'Political development' as mentioned, it is better to assess the contribution of the Universities to India's political development during the last fifty years and so. The fact is that the Universities being an autonomous bodies/centres of learning, i.e. teaching, research and extension, laying down a widely acceptable set of guidelines for detailed action on all these fronts, are set up by an acts of both the Parliament and the state legislatures and also enjoy a great deal of autonomy. But the fact is also true that the eradication of poverty, social, political and economic inequalities, unemployment, exploitation of the poor/ weaker sections by the rich/well-to-do persons, equal distribution of income, benefits of development and provision of right to work, which are the essential themes of political development, are beyond the scopes of the Universities. Because all these questions/issues are a power questions rooted in the development model, the country has adopted, and the socio-economic power structure that obtains in the country. What is needed is a fundamental change in the west model of political development adopted by the poor countries including India. So, the poor nations including India redefine their goals of development. As Kenneth Boulding writes correctly, "the presently underdeveloped countries are not going to develop. There is not enough of anything. There is not enough copper. There is not enough of an enormous number of elements which are essential to the development of economy. Economic development is the process by which the evil day is brought closer when everything will be gone".[1] It is the time that the developing nations take this warning seriously and change their course of development.

Despite all this, the Universities play a vital role to an extent in the country's political development. Education/higher education being the prime determinant of political development, makes citizen better by reducing crime, overcoming delusion, inhibiting superstitions/premordial considerations and in general, enhancing social and economic order. It also instils in people and electorate a sense of objectivity, co-operation, sacrifice, patriotism and nationalism to 'help the political structure to function smoothly as well as to save the nation from disaster during national emergency and foreign invasion. The university education, thus, contributes to better citizenry, better civic attitudes, deference to political independence, democratic values, contempt for feudalism and colonialism, and the ability to understand the rationality or irrationality of Government behaviour. Besides, political capacity manifestly depends on modern education. Higher education helps resolving the two most important problems in political modernisation namely, the changing of attitudes and reducing the gap between the ruling elites and the less modernised masses. Literacy as well as attitudes congruent with modernisation is crucial for effective political penetration by government as well as for meaningful citizenship. It also plays a role in societal adaptation to increasing role of specialization and structural differentiation in the achievement of political capacity, and in the progressive attainment of equality. The impact of the university education on political development and its various aspects such as political recruitment, political integration, political communication, interest articulation and aggregation and several types of political relations and on political ideology and secularism is believed to be very important. Research also stresses the role of the university education in legitimization. of the power structure, social *status quo*, political ideologies and colonial policies. On the basis of these considerations, there are some indicators and ingredients of political development namely political democracy, political stability or destabilization. political rights, civil liberties and human freedom which are given explicit preferences by most modern welfare states. Higher education, thus contributes to the development of these ingredients. For example. the fact is that the expansion of education, particularly higher education led to demand for political independence in this country and also in the several erstwhile British colonies.

Democracy being a simple indicator of political development requires literate masses/educated electorate for its success and smooth functioning. Because education has a number of effects on individuals that make the introduction and retention of democratic political systems likely. There is an impressive example that Japan ranks at the top not only in Asia but also in the whole world in terms of political democracy. It also has the highest literacy rate and the highest schooling levels. Besides, political stability is also necessary for political development. Educated citizens may act as a catalytic force for political stability and peace to an extent. It increases people's knowledge of the behaviour of the government and its policies. But it is to be noted that educated unemployed youth force poses a big threat to the stability of the government. The universities being a non-political entities having no governmental power/sanction cannot bring the unemployed youths to productive labour/work. The universities in this country do not have a manpower planning function. Undoubtedly, a major contribution of the universities in their transmission of knowledge is to prepare students for employment and service to the nation. However, it is suggested that the more education in the population the more is the stability of the society in terms of its political activities.

The level of political development and well-being of the people in this country is also judged in terms of political liberties and civil rights. Civil rights are essential conditions of a civilized society and political development. Without them, both are not possible. Political liberties mean the power of the people to be active in the affairs of the state. In other words, political liberty also empowers the citizens to play a role in determining who governs their country and what the laws will be. So, the democratic states value them greatly and provide safeguards against their encroachment either by the government or by individuals. They, thus, constitute the right of justice. But it is, widely believed that illiteracy and low levels of education and fulfilment of civil rights and political freedoms do not go hand in hand. These democratic freedoms are of little benefit to the Indian masses if they are to remain uneducated and the number of illiterates remain high. Illiterate and uneducated masses can be easily kept ignorant of their constitutional freedoms – civil and political. Violation of these rights is also not resented by an illiterate and uneducated people. But this is less possible in democratic societies characterised by educated and vigilant citizenry. However, it is noted that political and civil liberties do not seem to be closely related with literacy. Higher educational attainment of the people seems to matter a lot in making these political freedoms meaningful/ positive towards attaining socio-economic freedom which may be possible by equalising educational opportunities. Briefly, the political development of this country depends primarily on the quality and effectiveness of men and women.

Human development is incomplete without human freedom. Higher education leads to more human freedom, and in turn, human freedom leads to more demand for education. Thus, interrelationship is very strong. As regards the effects of education on human freedom, educated people may value human freedom more than illiterates. An educated masses may insist on justice and may fight for decent conditions of human living with dignity. Human freedom is, thus, strongly related with development of education. Education, if it is to be meaningful and fruitful, should help one to live a full life. It should be a continuous and life long affair. The universities should try to promote and strengthen appropriate attitudes, scientific-temper, respect of the diversity of cultures and dignity and freedom of the individuals and also the citizens to adapt traditional values to the new conditions that are evolving as regards political development in this country.

But it has been experienced that political freedoms and human freedom/rights appear to be meaningless especially for the poor, deprived and vulnerable Indian masses for want of economic freedom/justice, though the universities and colleges have been imparting education in Arts, Science, Commerce and professions since the country's independence. Higher education can neither; create a spirit of inquiry regarding the achievements of these political freedoms nor create a power of questioning the validity of political system, social traditions and social institutions in the minds of such people. As is true, these political freedoms and safeguard of human rights cannot be provided for those uneducated, illiterate, deprived exploited and neglected living below the poverty line, due to India being, a capitalist oriented, class divided, caste ridden and multi-religious society. Division of society into different classes being a feature of the capitalist society is a barrier to both social and political justice.

Besides, tertiary education plays a pivotal role in the process of political development of the country which includes social, economic and cultural development. It is at this level that all the generalists and specialists required for manning key positions in productive enterprises, research, administration, planning and education are trained in variety of ways. The character and quality of education provided at the University level play a major role in creating an ethos favourable to development, both individual and social. Directly, as well indirectly, the Universities influence a nation's endeavour in all the spheres of education, from that of the child to that of the adult, and in dissemination of education and culture to the people at large. The creative work of young students, scholars and teachers representing many disciplines has a great potential in laying bare the intricate social, economic, scientific and technological problems of growth and development and in finding solutions to these problems. By advancement and application of knowledge, the Universities also help in raising the prestige of a country and people amongst the nations of the world; enabling them to influence the course of events far beyond their own boundaries.

The primary function of the Universities is to provide a learning circumstances to a person so that he may be able to cultivate his mind, skills and character in order to lead a purposeful life and contribute to the well-being and growth of the society around him. It is helpful, even without going into many details, to visualise a number of competencies befitting specific objectives which may be desirable to cultivate through the educational process, competencies such as :

(i) Mainly on the cognitive side-knowledge of facts, phenomena and theories, understanding and application of this knowledge to new and unknown situations; ability to gather knowledge through first hand study of books as well as situations; to analyse and creatively synthesise thoughts and ideas;

(ii) Mainly on the side of skills-ability to observe, explore and experiment, competence to present and discuss ideas, to give and obtain co-operation in a team, to organise work and people for carrying out tasks undertaken; and

(iii) Mainly on the effective side-resourcefulness, self-reliance, capacity for disciplined hard work, sense of responsibility and inclination towards justice, fairplay and helpfulness towards others, lack of prejudice or prejudgement in all spheres, initiative and openness to change and experience.[2]

The Universities help strengthening national integration by creating understanding and fellow-feeling among their different groups, regional groups—both teachers and students which will be to throw up a political elite being capable of fixing up desirable national goals, evolving institutions through which these national goals can most successfully be obtained. Character-building among the students is also considered as a significant role. These certainly strengthen the ingredients of political development. But what is experienced in this country is that the teachers educate but pay little attention to character-building. The University education inculcates in people the knowledge of state and government, imparts training to people to become good citizens and also to make them conscious of social objectives, helps administrators, leaders, statesmen and diplomats to acquire a sound knowledge of the disciplines of Political Science and Public Administration to perform their functions efficiently, enables the students of these disciplines to find out the causes of corruption and expose injustice degenerating human society and suggest their remedies and due to the growth of nationalism and democracy encourages more people to actively participate in the political affairs of their respective states.

It is now universally recognised that education is both means as well as the end result of development. It is one of the basic needs of the people and their rights. Finally education is the most powerful instrument for the empowerment of the people. But it is to be noted that education system in India is in a very bad shape. Article 46 of the Indian Constitution provides that the state shall promote with special care the educational interest of weaker sections of the people, and in particular of the scheduled castes and scheduled tribes.

Inspite of the obligation assumed by the state, there is little evidence of the equalisation of the educational opportunity in our grossly unequal society. Infact, the gap in the educational opportunity is widening. The highest incidence of illiteracy is still among the these weaker sections of society. Women and the girls have the least educational opportunities in India. There cannot be any hope for achieving an egalitarian educational structure in India unless vastly expanded and improved educational opportunities are provided for these groups. Myron Weiner in his article published in the *Economic and Political Weekly* writes, "Deep class/caste divisions have been barriers to the development of national drive for mass education by those who have made it to the upper strata. It will take a major coalition of locally based groups, active participation of media, the contribution of researchers, the support of investors, educators, social activists and trade unions to get India to address the way it treats the children of poor".[3] This issue causes concern to higher education in the country.

In this context the Kothari Commission's considered observations on the issue of equalising educational opportunities may be recalled. "One of the important social objectives of education is to equalise opportunity, enabling the backward or under privileged classes and individuals to use education as a lever for the improvement of their condition. Every society, that values social justice and is anxious to improve the lot of the common man and cultivate all available talent, must ensure progressive equality of opportunity to all sections of the population. This is the only guarantee for building up an equalitarian and human society in which the exploitation of the weak will be minimised".[4] Briefly, the realisation of the commission's objectives into practice to an extent, definitely strengthens the political capability of the Indian society, making the ingredients of political development meaningful and fruitful for the greatest good of the greatest number especially the poor/ disadvantaged/neglected/exploited sections of the Indian population.

NOTES

1. S.P. Verma, Theories of Political Development : A Critic and Search for an Alternative Approach (in) *Political Science Review*, Quarterly Journal of the Department of Political Science, University of Rajasthan, Jaipur, Vol. 16, No.2, April-June, 1977, pp. 16-17.
2. Rais Ahmed, Universities: Perspectives and Problems (in) *Mainstream*, Vol. XX, No. 23, February 6, 1982, pp 13-14, New Delhi.
3. R.N. Prasad, Conflicts arising out of Contradictions in Indian Political System – Their Implications for Internal Security, (this lecture/paper presented/delivered at the 145 Internal Security Course for Deputy Superintendent of Police and Assistant Commandant of CPOS at Internal Security Academy, Central Reserve Police Force, Mount Abu, Rajasthan, 2-4, August, 1997, pp. 10-11 (unpublished).
4. S.V. Chittibabu, Higher Education: Some Paradoxes and Dilemmas (in) *J.N.U. News,* Vol. XI, October 1990, No. 10, New Delhi, p 18.

12

SOCIO-POLITICAL DEVELOPMENT IN INDIA DURING THE LAST FIFTY YEARS

PREAMBLE TO THE CONSTITUTION

"We, the people of India, having solemnly resolved to constitute India into a Sovereign Socialist Secular Democratic Republic and to secure to all its citizens :

JUSTICE, social economic and political;

LIBERTY of thought, expression, belief, faith and worship;

EQUALITY of status and of opportunity; and to promote among them all;

FRATERNITY assuring the dignity of the individual and the Unity and integrity of the Nation;

....do hereby adopt, enact and give to ourselves this Constitution".

India became free from the British Colonial rule from 15th August, 1947. The Constitution for Independent India was prepared and finalised after wide consultation with a cross-section of the people. The Constitution was inaugurated on 26th January, 1950 and it came into force from the same day.

Fifty years have passed since India became a Republic. Its GOLDEN JUBILEE all over the country which coincides with the celebration of new millennium. This is a moment consecrated by history. We all rejoice in the great achievements of the people of India.

The word 'Republic' in a political term, signifies that the governance of the country is through elected representatives of the people. It also means a form of government in which the people or their elected representatives possess the supreme power.

During the last fifty years of Indian, independence, India itself and the world have witnessed profound changes – changes that have affected the very structure of human thought and action. In this chapter, it is attempted to make a glimpse of events or changes which have taken place during the last fifty years with special reference to social-political developments in India.

Indian Society

India has a multi-caste society. The term 'Caste' is derived from the Portuguese word 'Casta' meaning breed, race, kind. Today, it is employed to define a concept of Hinduism. An indigenous word for caste is '*jati*' or '*zat*'. Caste is an endemic feature of Hindu life. However, it has now effectively pervaded all stratas of our society so much so that it is found among other religious orders like the Muslims, Sikhs and Christians. E. Blunt defines caste as an endogamous group, bearing a common name, membership of which is heareditary, imposing on its members certain restrictions in matters of social intercourse, either following a common traditional occupation or claiming a common origin, and generally regarded as forming a single homogeneous community.

Hindu society is classified into Brahmin – the priests; Kashatriya – the warriors; Vaishya – the traders; Sudras – the slaves; Pancham (outcaste) – the aboriginal/unicivilized tribes. Eighty per cent of India's population lives in villages where life is traditionally narrowly circumscribed. It is in the villages that the caste system, sanctioned by Hindu tradition, has its most powerful hold. Members of each caste share, by tradition, a common lot and occupy by virtue of their birth, a defined status and role within the village society. It is estimated that there are more than 200 castes or '*jatti*' in

India. The caste system is paradoxically dubbed by Alan Beals as 'being together separately. Each caste or group with a well-developed life of its own, its membership by birth, a Brahmin at the head of social hierarchy, restrictions on feeding, on social intercourse, on choice of occupation and on marriage – all this corroborates the above definition.

The Constitution of India Republic ensures social justice to all its citizens (Preamble). Social justice means social equality, implying a social system where there are no special rights, no special privileges, no special dignities attached to a person on the basis of birth, caste or religion; equal opportunity for every citizen to develop his personality. Social justice also implies absence of distinction in social status of the people because of difference in race, religion, caste, sex and birth (Article 15 – Fundamental Rights).

What is important today is change in social values, social attitude and social institutions to achieve social justice. The basic thing is education. Education should create a spirit of enquiry in the minds of the people, and a power of questioning the validity of social traditions and social institutions under Indian Constitution. It is an irony that many of the unprivileged and outcaste people still are under the thick cloud of ignorance, illiteracy, obscurantism and illusion. By Article 17 of the Constitution untouchability is abolished and its practice in any form is prohibited. But in practice, it still continues to exist.

Social justice cannot be achieved in India because of capitalist-oriented, class-divided, caste-ridden and multi-religious society. Division of society into different classes, being a feature of the capitalist society, is a barrier to social justice. Forty-eight per cent of Indian population is under poverty line. The Directive Principles of State Policy (Articles 38 and 39) guarantee a social system in which social, political and economic justice will prevail and inequalities in status, facilities and opportunities will be eliminated. In the absence of economic justice and freedom, no social justice will emerge in India.

The Directive Principles of State Policy (Article 45 and 46) enjoin upon the State to provide for free and compulsory education for all children below fourteen years, that too within ten years of the Indian Republic, and also to promote the educational and economic interests of the weaker sections of the people, particularly the Scheduled Castes and the Scheduled Tribes. Despite all these ideals, illiteracy in India is highest among these weaker sections of the society. Barring some of the South Asian countries, India has the highest rate of illiteracy in the world. We cannot hope for an egalitarian educational structure in India unless vastly expanded and improved educational opportunities are provided for the weaker sections of the people. Education is both means as well as the end result of development. It is one of the basic needs of the people and their human right. It is the most powerful instrument for the empowerment of the people.

Caste and Politics

The actual operation of the democratic process in India has brought into sharp focus the complexity of the relationship between politics and society. The general feature of politics in democratic societies is that it intervenes to influence society and that it also reflects the social reality. It has been empirically observed that instead of playing an activist role in society, politics becomes passive and reflective of social forces. The activist and reflective roles of politics in society can lead to a conflict between politics and society. In this situation, India has been attempting a reconciliation between a modern democratic political system and a social system which has its firm foundations in ancient culture.

A specific feature of the development of contemporary Indian society is that all basic changes have been initiated by Indian states. The state is the agency of change in society, and for performing such a central role, the state seeks its legitimacy through the democratic verdict of the people. Politics in India is a pre-eminent factor in societal change, and this is responsible for the complexity of the interactions between politics and society.

Further, large masses of the people suffer from social and economic discriminations, and they look to the state functionaries for protection and survival. While those who belong to the vulnerable strata of society seek protection from the state, the privileged and powerful seek to control state institutions and resources for protection and promotion of their material interests. The essence of the struggle is – who can control state power through the democratic verdict of the people? The political parties and elections have thus assumed great importance in India because state power can be controlled only through democratically legitimized methods.

Caste as an Ideology in Politics

In India, caste is used by political parties for political mobilization and elections. It is maintained, for instance, that political parties have to operate in a given specific social milieu, and that social identities and categories of the people's loyalties are the basis on which politics has to operate. Since a social structure is based on caste and the caste structure determines the context of politics, the political parties cannot ignore this social reality or context.

Caste occupies a very important place in the politics of India at local and regional levels. It is traceable in various important events like selection of candidates for elective offices, formation of groups and factions, canvassing campaign, exercise of franchise, making of ministries, securing government favours and the like. Similar regard is paid when the list of political party's office-bearers is prepared. More so, when a single party is not in a position to have its own candidates, alliances are formed on the basis of caste. It is only in a strife-ridden situation that the unusual course of shaking off caste orientation is resorted to and of conscience vote is taken.

The politics of caste and communalism is supposed to have no room in a secular, democratic and socialist India. However, in practice, things are not so, caste politics has risen form ashes in a new form. It remains a central element of India's society even while adapting itself to the values and methods of democratic politics. Caste has a major role at the local and regional levels, it is marginal at the all-India level.

Caste politicisation can be viewed in a different perspective. Caste in the traditional sense should go. Caste in the modern sense should survive to exert a liberating influence. Caste politics which implies an institutional arrangement of bringing about political democracy inculcating egalitarian aspirations among the members of a particular group will become a mechanism exerting a liberating influence. Caste associations may play a vital role in the exercise of political freedom through groups. Direct election system and the growth of political parties have abetted caste consciousness and thereby promoted what the Constitution has really designed to defeat. Prof. Kothari visualises : 'By drawing the caste system into the web of organisation, politics finds material for its articulation and mould it into its own design'. However, caste politics that kills the spirit of an egalitarian society should be discarded.

Role of Class in Politics

The term 'class' is a heterogeneous group or organisation based on a specific interest, particularly economic. Like caste, the class has its own role to play in the political process of the country. The upper class (bourgeoisie) has been in a very decisive position in effecting the decision-making process after independence. The result is more and more economic degradation of the people and the emergence of social tensions and conflicts in the Indian political system. For instance, the democratic legitimacy of the leading classes is slowly eroding, and they seek the state power or coercion to meet the challenges of the deprived strata of society. Concentration of economic power into the hands of a few has been going on steadily in flagrant disregard to the ideals of economic justice contained in the Directive Principles of State Policy. The rich and landed class in rural areas have constituted rural bourgeoisie. A handful of people have secured possession over land. Nothing substantial has come out for the deprived class despite the abolition of *zamindari* system and the implementation of land reform laws. It is estimated that seventy per cent of the lower class people in rural areas are landless.

The system of mixed economy in India has been responsible for the incessant growth of economic power in the hands of the middle class (elite). The property owners in rural and urban areas are a minority and yet they have instruments to wield power and indulge in large scale exploitation. The elites maintain their status through various means–economic position, active participation in political parties, holding of important position in government departments. Indian capitalism still has retained considerable political power. This sort of uneasy relationship between the affluent minority and the poor and exploited people can be resolved either by a revolution against property owners or by suppression of the deprived people by coercive mechanism of the state.

It is, therefore, alleged that Indian democracy suffers from serious pitfalls. It is nothing less than plutocracy or role of wealthy people. Indian polity is democratic in principle, but in practice, it combines rule by the many and the few. Its distinctive feature is that permeating India's elaborate web of social hierarchy, there is systematic elitism which contravenes the nation's egalitarian Constitution.

Political Development

Alfred Diamont defines political development as 'a process by which a political system acquires an increased capacity to sustain successfully and continuously new types of goals and demands and the creation of new types of organizations'. It can also be defined as 'a process of meeting new goals and demands in a flexible manner'.

In the pre-independence India, that is during the freedom struggle, persons who were ready to make sacrifices joined politics. After independence, the general elections based on adult suffrage began to throw up new elements whose strongest qualifications lay in their acceptability by the newly enfranchised sections of the society. Politics has become election-based. It is through election that one now graduates in politics.

Before the 1967 general election, the Congress party which was national movement of pre-independence period, maintained its monolithic rule in India. But in the general elections of 1967, new forces registered their ascendancy and triumph. Coalition governments were formed in eight states – Punjab, Haryana, U.P., Bihar, Madhya Pradesh, Orissa, Kerala, and West Bengal. Though it formed the government at the Centre, the Congress party secured

40.8 per cent votes only in the Lok Sabha election. The year 1967 may thus rightly be said to constitute a 'Great Divide' in Indian political history.

The general elections of 1967 signified the dwindling of the old leadership and heralded the full emergence of a new leadership. As a result, the representatives became very nearly like those they represent. This has been inherent in the Indian political system. Under the Constitution of India, the source of political power became voting right and the majority. The hitherto neglected groups, which are backward and illiterate, but which nevertheless constitute majority in the country were bound to come increasingly into power.

The fourth general election of 1967 was followed and accompanied by some unusual events. Jawaharlal Nehru passed away before the fourth general election and his place was filled up by leadership which had no such charisma at least to begin with. It was also of economic hardship due to severe drought, devaluation of Indian currency which hit the economy very adversely. Elections were becoming increasingly expensive, much beyond the capacity of most politicians, which inevitably made them dependent on money bags of businessmen. This politics became a linkage politics. The adoption of planning and mixed economy pattern of development greatly expanded the patronage of the state. The businessman needs the politician to help him in getting various kinds of benefits from government. In the process, a new relationship of inter-dependencies and mutual benefits was created.

In short, electoral politics was beginning to produce its own logic, and it became the seed-bed of corruption involving the politician, the fund-givers, and even the voters. Politics has been fast becoming amoral, if not immoral also at times. Politics has become a power game and it seeks its very legitimacy from elections. The profile of the Indian politician has thus been changing. The present day politician is not a continuation of the generation of freedom fighters.

The Indian society itself has been witnessing a massive shifts in its value system, orientations and attitudes. It has become aggressively materialistic in its outlook. Selfishness today stalks the land. The prevalent motto appears to be plainly and unashamedly 'self before society'. Values and graces of life have all but disappeared. Laws of the land are getting increasingly violated with impunity, especially by those who constitute the power structure or have access to it. There is no organised citizen power or public opinion upholding the higher values of life. In fine, the society itself has become corrupt, sick, baseless and normless. Religion had in the past regulated to an extent the social behaviour. But the way secularism has been interpreted in India has removed the fear of God from the minds of many people. A large part of the society has a very faint ethical sensitivity.

Impact of the New Forces

The political system of India is of late finding itself under mounting stress, and what is more, there does not appear to be any signs of pressures getting abatted in the near future. Firstly, the country's politics seeks to entrust more and more activities and functions to the state. Second, there is too much of demand being made on the country' political system with little attention being given to its capabilities and capacities. Third, all sectors of the people in India have become increasingly politicised though not equally and in well-rounded form. Fourth, politics has become growingly ruthless and normless. Success is in total disregard to how it is achieved and by what means. Fifth, politics has been becoming increasingly a historical, being conducted too much in terms of the present and discounting the future. Sixth, politics has become increasingly agitational creating an impression that it pays – or, as someone said, it alone pays these days. Seventh, politics has generated a steep deterioration in moral values. Political opportunism is a widespread evil debasing the country's politics. Eighth, political corruption, money or patronage has become the most serious feature of Indian politics. Ninth, the ubiquitousness of politics in India is quite worrying today. Politics seems to pervade most areas of life. It superimposes itself on almost everything. The dwindling concern for the nation, the deterioration of public ethics and its incapacity to control population growth are other forces of stress in the Indian political system.

We have discussed some of the negative effects of political development in India. In spite of occasional ups and downs, India's achievements have certainly been many and impressive though not adequate and very wide-ranging. Viewed from the indicators or measures, of varying reliability of political development, the performance of Indian polity after independence has been quite encouraging. Main positive indicators may involve national integration, voters turnout, popular participation in governmental decision-making process, autonomous interest groups, mass media circulation, political and administrative decentralization, autonomy of local government institutions and quasi-governmental sectors, stable party system, political competitiveness, consensual politics, openness in public administration, provision for redressal of public grievances, freedom of the press, education and urbanization. The negative indicators of political development such as political coup, riots, political prisoners and political assassination and manipulated defection of legislators have been experienced in the country. However, in degree or extent, they have not been beyond control. Unlike our neighbouring countries, the political coup has not raised its head in India.

A profile of fifty years of the functioning of democratic, secular, federal and activist political system in India reveals its positive and negative features, its achievements and failures, and on the basis of such a dialectical understanding of the last fifty years, the emerging tendencies and trends can summarily be emphasized.

The most important achievement of Indian political system is the holding of periodical elections on the basis of universal adult franchise and at regular intervals. The impact of elections on Indian society has been qualitative, the percentage of voter's turnout has been satisfactory. Gradually the voters have started evaluating governmental performances, the distance between government and the voters has narrowed down, competition in politics has been legitimized, and gradually the secular source of power has emerged as a new factor in Indian society. Participatory politics has raised the level of political awareness of the masses and government has become a critical factor in voter's life. In spite of a slow process as also the revealed negative features, by all standard, adult franchise has been a revolutionary social factor in India. Politicisation of an indifferent and apathetic community is the first step towards democratic advancement of a society, and elections have achieved this in India.

One significant achievement of Indian polity in the last fifty years has been party alternation and peaceful transition from a defeated party to an electorally successful groups of a party. People's verdict in the 1977 general election was accepted by the hitherto ruling Congress party without any resistance. India is an important member of international community, and its counsels receive serious attention in various countries. India is one of the pioneers of the non-alignment movement. It has managed its economy fairly well. India also ranks as the tenth most highly industrialised country in the world. Other attainments of the political system in India can be summed up as follows – Its unbroken continuity of the polity. The constitution is functioning well, a fairly stable government at the centre and in the states, peaceful change of government strictly through ballots, a steady deepening of political awareness of the people, and democratic institutions taking roots at all levels.

We will now discuss some of the relevant points and salient features of political developments in independent India in different spheres such as political party system, election system, national integration, centre-state relation, coalition and minority governments, etc.

Political Parties

India has a multi-party system. Majority parties are operating at the national level. There are several parties operating at regional level, local level, and other minor parties or fringe organizations with limited area of operation. The number of parties and organizations operating in India at various levels is estimated to be more than two hundred. These big and small parties or organizations appear on the political scene at election time. In India, the political party pre-supposes participation in power.

India has more or less a single-dominant-party system as far as the national scene is concerned. Congress party alone has an India-wide effective network by virtue of which it has managed to remain in power. Being the national movement in the freedom struggle, Congress party is secular, non-communal and socialistic maintaining plurality within itself which makes it more representative, providing flexibility and sustaining internal competition. Indian people's commitment towards a party or some parties is not rigid. They want a stable and democratic system. So they naturally prefer a party that can give them a stable administration subscribing to the norms of democracy, secularism and socialism. They also look at the better prospects of a particular party and for this reason, Congress has an edge over all other parties.

Political parties are the life-lines of Indian politics. A noteworthy feature of the country's party system is its extreme fluidity which owes itself to a craving for office in some party or the other. Ironically, there are more leaders than the number or offices which will absorb them, and this results in the proliferation of parties in India. A regretful feature of Indian political parties is their occasional splits and break-ups the primary motivation of which being more personal than ideological. Most of the parties have not escaped a split. Congress party's first split in 1969 followed by the second split in 1978, the Janata party's division in 1979 necessitating the mid-term general election in 1980 in which the heroes of 1977election were made to eat the dust, the Communist party split in 1964 into three groups, and the state level party DMK split resulting in the emergence of AIADMK in Tamil Nadu can be mentioned in point.

Because of the pre-dominance of Congress party in India, the term 'opposition' used to be applied to refer to all non-Congress parties. One characteristic of the opposition parties is lack of perceptible degree of responsibility. The opposition in India is highly fragmented and weak and consequently irresponsible and ineffective despite it being generally noisy. Even when the opposition parties could combine to dislodge the Congress at the Centre, Janata party in 1977, Janata Dal alias the National Front in 1989, the United Front in 1996, BJP-led Coalition in 1998, there could not be coherence among them. As a result, the government felt necessitating mid-term general elections.

Other characteristics of Indian political parties are – absence of ideological orientation in most of the major parties, not the principle but personalities having the determining influence; the emergence of some regional parties with a distinct parochial or communal character generating tendencies opposed to the forces of nationalism, democracy and socialism; absence of commitment to discipline; the rise and fall of minor political parties or organizations creating a very confusing spectacle. Political parties are not evolving along healthy lines. The spirit if service has given way to the craze for power. The goal is to capture power, by hook or by crook. The opposition parties, lacking a sense of responsibility, do not follow the rules of the game. What is needed today in India is a healthier system of political parties. A new mechanism has to be evolved to contain a tendency or voluptuous motivation to raise parties which of late has a close link with the system of coalition government for the sake of sharing power.

Elections

Since the enforcement of the Constitution of India, the general elections of Lok Sabha have taken place thirteen times. The voter's turnout was lowest in the first election of 1952 (45.7%), and highest in 1994 election (64%). The hitherto dominant Congress party was dislodged by the Janata party in 1977 which secured 43.17 per cent of votes against Congress vote 34.5 per cent. In the 1989 election, the Congress again failed to form the government securing only 197 votes. The Janata Dal-led National Front government was formed. This general election was the most ambivalent poll verdict since independence. The people knew which party they were rejecting, but were not secure as to which party they were accepting. They wanted a change from Congress government to a non-Congress one. The outcome of the 1991 general election of Lok Sabha was a hung Parliament. However, the largest single party Congress capturing 221 seats formed the government with the support of some other secular party members.

In the general election of 1996, the BJP and its allies pushed the mighty Congress to second place by winning 187 seats, and formed the government at the Centre which lasted exactly 13 days. With the fall of the BJP-led government, some secular parties in the Lok Sabha combined and formed a new parliamentary party called 'United Front'. The UF formed the government with outside support of Congress party, but it also fell when Congress withdrew its support resulting in a mid-term general election in 1998. In the 1998 election, BJP retained its status as the single largest party in the 12th Lok Sabha. The BJP-led government was formed which lasted nearly one year. The coalition being loose, the government fell or was voted out of power on the floor of parliament by one vote resulting in the mid-term election of 13th Lok Sabha in 1999. In the last general election of 1999, the BJP and its allies formed a formidable alliance known as National Democratic Alliance (NDA), and won absolute majority to form the government.

We can thus see that political disasters have befallen Congress party since 1977. The main factor responsible for the electoral debacle of Congress party in 1977 was the national Emergency Rule of 1975. Two factors were responsible for the Congress defeat in 1989 – the autocratic rule of Rajiv Gandhi and a strong opposition to the dynastic rule of Nehru family within and outside the Congress party. The poor performance of Congress Party in the next four general elections has been due, to a certain extent, to the weak leadership with decreased charisma and the better composition of the fragmented opposition parties to dislodge Congress party. Notwithstanding the salutary provision of the Constitution, our electoral processes have been considerably polluted by what is called the role of money power, muscle power and the mafia gangs. Electoral reform with more independent power given to the Election Commission is most needed today.

Since 1967, coalition government has been a regular feature of Indian polity, at least at state level. Its result is a mushroom increase in political parties or organizations because even small parties can get a change of sharing power with bigger parties. We have experienced a minority government too either at national level or at the state level. Here the parties supporting the ruling party from outside enjoy power and influence without responsibility. So far as national integration is concerned, the principle of 'unity in diversity' still holds good in India. As for the centre-state relations, the critiques of some state leaders deserve serious consideration.

The via media of the problem seems to be more powers devolved to states without attenuating a strong centre.

In our celebration of Indian Republic's Golden Jubilee, we cannot but remember India's great leaders of freedom movement who sacrificed their everything for the nation – Mahatma Gandhi, Pandit Jawaharlal Nehru and many others. We have been reaping the fruits of their hard labour and sacrifice so much so that India has become the largest democracy in the world. If we look around, we can see many countries, far and near, where might and not right rules today. The fact that India has been free and safe from catastrophe is the result of Mahatma Gandhi's principle of non-violence in the freedom struggle. We think the Almighty God has vindicated the Mahatma's good and long-lasting policy in this generation.

Mahatma Gandhi was a revolutionary – unique among revolutionaries. He marched for freedom, clad in the robe of truth, with non-violence for his staff. He did not counter the violence of the oppressor with the violence of the oppressed. He met it by changing the oppressed form within. He freed them from fear and hatred. He ignited the greatest peaceful mass movement known to history. At his gentle summons, millions of Indians rose to assert their human dignity and walked upright with the spark of greatness in them. The most suitable memorial of Mahatma Gandhi is to follow his great teachings and to organise works in order to further his constructive ideas in the development of the nation.

SELECT READINGS

Bhambhri, C.P., *Politics in India*, Vikas, New Delhi, 1988.

Hartman, Horst, *Political Parties in India*, Meenakshi Prakashan, Meerut (1971)

Indian Journal of Political Science - IPSA, Oct-Dec., 1980.

India Today, March 16, 1998: *Politics India,* January, 1998.

Johri, J.C., *Indian Politics*, Vishal Publications, New Delhi,1987.

Maheshwari, S.R., *Political Development in India*, Concept Publishing Company, New Delhi, 1984.

Mathur, P.C., *Social Bases of Indian Politics*, Aalekh Publishers, Jaipur, 1984.

Prasad, R.N., Conflicts arising out of Contradictions in Indian Political System–Their Implications for Internal Security –Article (Lecture delivered in the 145 Internal Security Course for Dy. SPs and Assistant Commandant of CPO's at *Internal Security Academy*, CRPF, Mount Abu (Rajasthan) 2-4/8/1994 (unpublished).

Subrahmanya, *Development of Politics in India*.

13

JUDICIAL ACTIVISM, LEGISLATURE AND THE COMMON MAN

It was an antique Venice. Time had parked itself in the portico of 1594. In the serene morn of the day sat a Court of Justice. The solemn proceedings as well as the pronouncement were in the catchy language of literature. Inside the august dome was reeling in echo the young Judge's proverbial pronouncement.

> "This bond is forfeit;
> And lawfully by this the Jew may claim
> A pound of flesh."

The proceedings were austere. The terms and conditions of the bond were more than clear. Under the general rules of construction, a pound of flesh must have included the blood involved. But it was the Judge who, moved by her conscience and commitment to a greater justice, not so warranted under the law or the contract either, declared the bond inoperative not in law but for the purposes of execution. Perhaps this was a unique dispensation of a judicial activist! The pronouncements were simple but classic. Even a naive could follow. The activism is understood by all including the beneficiary. Back to the Indian reality from Shakespearian fiction, in 1890's Justice Syed Mahmood, the first Indian Judge of the Allahabad High Court (formerly N.W. Province High Court), expounded that law as a science would be unworthy of the name, if it did not to some extent provide the means of preventing the mischiefs of improvidence, rashness, blind confidence and credulity on one side, and skill, avarice, cunning and a gross violation of the principles of morals and conscience on the other. Thus going beyond the textual confinement of law, he held in the case of Queen Emperor *vs.* Pohpi and Ors. that an appeal under section 420 of the Code of Criminal Procedure could not be disposed of in the absence of the accused, and the appellant must be heard in person. And perhaps first sowed the seed of judicial activism in India. The precise issue before the court was whether a court could decide the case of the under-trial when he was neither present nor represented by any lawyer, by merely looking into the case-record. Justice Mahmood ruled that the pre-condition of the case, being "heard", could be fulfilled only when somebody speaks.

The expression 'judicial activism' suffers from patent absurdity, as its contrary leads to nothing except 'judicial passivism or inaction'. Rather, it may better be construed as action of a judicial activist. The concept of "judicial activism" was given birth by Pro. Shapiro while classifying the judges into two broad groups— Judicially Modest and Judicially activist – on the basis of their tendency to interfere with the policy of any government or otherwise. As put by Justice Hidayatullah, apart from the decision of disputes between litigating parties, the task of Judiciary is to keep the other two limbs of administration within the limits of their powers under the Constitution. According to him, this and the next task of expounding the meaning behind the words of the Constitution and the laws are the two important functions of thc Judiciary. Ordinarily, whenever the Judiciary step: beyond the limits of these functions, to discharge social justice or judicial justice and commits to the process of social engineering, it is labelled as Judicial Activism. In most of the cases, the approaches differ; tendencies differ; frames of mind distinguish and tag brands. Some of the judges confine themselves to the written words of law, while some others consider that written words of law, though intended to avoid confusion, are often the mother of confusions surrounding it. Some exhibit an inclination to go strictly by the legislative intent behind a law, while some others tend to go beyond in search of social aspect of law, its effectiveness in preserving the social order, in ensuring the rights of an individual in the society he lives and also in securing a better society. In many cases the judges are guided by the concept of social justice and exhibit a growing shift from granting mere individualistic or legal justice to rendering social justice and 'judicial justice'. Judges are no more and no less than human beings brought up and carried with their individual values, social experiences, respective cultural base and attitudinal behaviour. Measured by these, judges are classified as either radical or conservative. From this viewpoint, judicial activism is synonymous to judicial radicalism. Thanks to Glendom Schubert! On the basis of their inclination to uphold the policies of government and law-making bodies as true reflective or so, judges are sometimes branded as either Committed or Uncommitted. Judicial activism in such cases is construed as opposed to committed judiciary. Any intervention by judiciary in the sphere of the Executive or the Legislature – even though permitted under the Constitutional Scheme is now-a-days commonly termed as Judicial Activism. Bal Krishna, the noted law critic, has described the concept of judicial activism as reflecting of the following trends, viz. Expansion of rights of hearing in the administrative process; excessive delegation without limitation, expansion of judicial control over discretionary power, expansion of judicial review over the administration, promotion of open government, exercise of indiscriminate contempt power, exercise of non-existent jurisdiction, and extending the standard rules of interpretation in its search for achieving economic, social and educational objectives and passing of orders which are *per se* unworkable or implicate state finance. The judiciary under its powers of judicial review examines the Acts of Parliament, the legislatures and acts of government and other administrative bodies. Much of the judicial activism is expressed by the superior courts, i.e. the Courts of Record or the Courts of Constitutional Writ jurisdiction like Supreme Court and High Courts of India, through their powers of judicial review. The degree or velocity of Judicial activism is accordingly measured in terms of frequency of exercise of this power as it is normally understood.

Jurists and legal experts are sharply divided on this. Judge Learned Hand, Prof. Shapiro and others viewed that as judges who do not derive their powers directly from the people and are not responsible to them, they are not justified in multiplying the acts of political agencies like legislature and government, who derive their powers directly from the people. According to them, judicial activism leads to question about neutrality of judges too. On the other hand, according to Prof. Wechler, Bickel, Black and others, if the power of judicial review flows from the Constitution itself, then it is quite justified and the Constitutional functions of the courts is to define values and proclaim, principles, which should be in the field of exceedingly few matters. They further argued that the judicial activism by way of rational exercise of the powers of judicial review was justified for 'legitimating a legislative measure'. This controversy started in USA in 1803 and continued for years without any final opinion. In the opinion of Justice M. Hidayatullah, the controversy that has been going on in India since 1950 itself, between the judiciary, legislature and executive is precisely arising from the decision of disputes between litigating parties, the task of the judiciary is to keep the other two limbs of administration, i.e. legislature and executive within the respective limits of their powers under the Constitution. According to him, the task of expounding the meaning behind the words of the Constitution and the laws is the most important function of the Indian judiciary. The construction and interpretation of the Constitution and the laws being a delicate task, under the Constitutional scheme, the High Courts and finally the Supreme Court have been reckoned as having the last say in discovering the meaning. In fact, growing tendency to disagree to this Constitutional position has led to an unwarranted confrontation between the judiciary on one hand and the legislature and the executive on the other. The confrontation between the judiciary and the executive is not new. It is understood too. The separation and division of powers which Montesquieu had considered to be an effective safeguard of personal liberty and freedom gradually seemed to be less evident as the executive, meaning the Council of Ministers in practice, resorted to influence the legislature, and the legislative wing in turn tries to restrict the Judiciary. This trend resulted in inevitable thrust on the executive which, however, finds the task too great, partly because the legislature is 'continually making, unmaking and altering the laws made by itself' – which results in multiplicity and complexity of laws and also ambiguity, and partly because of supplementation of such laws by the judiciary by their judicial law making and growing intervention in matters not involving strictly any point of law. It is said that, in principle, judicial intervention should not occur unless a point of law needs to be settled; but in practice, when courts give direction in such circumstances, most often crisis becomes more complicated, controversies still not cleared and contentions unresolved. Instances of judicial activism in India are many. According to many, judicial activism is primarily not a consequence of executive inaction, as the malaise seemed to have stemmed from the executive's desire 'to co-opt the courts into promoting its vision of social order.' On the other hand, the confrontation between the judiciary and the legislature is a long history in England, but the growing cases of confrontation between the judiciary and the legislature in India, almost on misconception in many cases, is the most notable feature and of grave public concern today. The judicial activism in India has assumed a very different dimension from this angle.

The actual root of the problem was unmistakably diagnosed by Justice Hidayatullah long back in 1975. In his estimate, the Parliament used to pass sixty Acts at an average every year from 1950 and the Legislatures of the States also seemed to be equally prolific, thereby pouring out statutes, rules and regulations in thousands every year requiring the people to do this and not to do that. For almost every contingency, a law is made and before the ink is dry, it needs amendment. It is often found that retrospective laws are passed either to by-pass or undermine or to overrule decisions of courts. If society changes, laws must necessarily change, but society has not changed so greatly as the laws, it is viewed. No doubt, a written Constitution is reckoned as forming the fundamental and paramount law of the nation and consequently an Act of any legislature, repugnant to the Constitution becomes void and the courts are called upon to declare so. In this way, more and more, law is becoming "a weapon to fight conflicting interests and the court is becoming the arena." Both the legislature and the judiciary are much less consciously drawn to confrontation.

The second field where the confrontation is also on steep increase relates to legislative privileges and the legislature's attempt to exercise unrestricted judicial powers. Like in U.K., Parliamentary privileges are not codified in India too. Under the Constitution, powers, privileges and immunities of Parliament or a State legislature, as the case may be, and of the members and the committees thereof are such as may from time to time be defined by law by Parliament or State Legislature concerned, but until so defined, should be those of the House of Commons of United Kingdom and of its members and committees, at the commencement of the Constitution, i.e. on 26th January, 1950. The Constitution does not exhaustively lay down the legislative privileges. While clause (1) of Article 194 of the Constitution confers freedom of speech on legislators independently of anything in Article 19(1)(a), subject to Articles 208 and 211 and Rules of Procedure read with standing orders of the Legislative Assembly concerned, clause (2) of Article 194 goes one step further by conferring total immunity on a legislator from any local proceedings even if his speech on the floor of the House concerned violates the fundamental right of any other person as available under Article 19(1)(a) and transgresses any other provision of the Constitution, like Art. 211. According to the Supreme Court and the Constitutional experts, this immunity is complete and is based on the principle that it is in essence of the Parliamentary system of government that people's representatives should be free to express themselves without fear of legal consequences. Clause (3) of Article 194 confers other powers, privileges and immunities as enjoyed by the House of Commons in the United Kingdom as on 26th January, 1950 on the State Legislatures until defined by legislation. These other privileges include, *inter alia*, that whenever someone commits contempt of any State legislature or breach of any privilege since enjoyed by any member of such legislature, the latter can act as court and award punishment. However, the punitive powers of any State legislature have so far remained undefined. It is strange that the legislatures in India have failed in enacting laws codifying their privileges, for almost half a century of the working of the Constitution in spite of the wishes of the framers of the Constitution. So, as of now, the legislatures in India derive their privileges from two sources – the Indian Constitution and the British Convention.

The privileges of the House of Commons are many and varied,

the most controversial of which is empowering the Speaker to summon a person for alleged breach of privilege of the House of its member. The Speaker may admonish, reprimand and even sentence the guilty to imprisonment. By the British convention, as they do not have any written Constitution like ours, the judiciary does not intervene unless the order of arrest is a non-speaking order.

The biggest confrontation in India between the judiciary and the legislature in this field thus centres around the judicial interference with undefined parliamentary privileges and powers to punish for contempt, which subsequently assumed an ugly shape of the issue : Who is superior – Judiciary or Legislature! The first ever confrontation between the judiciary and the legislature in India arose in 1954 over the privilege issue when the Speaker of the U.P. Assembly ordered the detention of Mr. H.D. Mistry, Deputy editor of Blitz, on the charge of committing a breach of privilege. The Speaker's action was challenged before the Supreme Court which held that detention of a person in custody without producing him before any magistrate within 24 hours of the arrest amounted to a clear violation of Article 22(2) of the Constitution. However, the preliminary question raised by the U.P. Assembly as to whether the Assembly should entertain the notices of the Court, respond to it and be represented before the court remained undecided. The controversy resurfaced in 1959 before the Supreme Court in the case of M.S.M. Sharma *vs.* V.K. Sinha, in which the court had to decide whether the publication of an expunged portion of the Bihar Assembly proceedings in *Searchlight*; a news bulletin, constituted a breach of privilege or not. The Supreme Court in a very cautious approach to the issue this time ruled that the privileges enjoyed by the Parliament and the State legislatures, on the analogy of the House of Commons, were not subject to Article 19(1)(a) of the Constitution, and that the Assembly was within its jurisdiction to prohibit publication of any report of its debates, even if the prohibition contravened the Fundamental Right to freedom of expression and speech. A worse confrontation between the U.P. Assembly and the judiciary surfaced again in 1964 relating to one Keshav Singh. The facts were that Keshav Singh had been found guilty of contempt of the U.P. Legislature and had been produced under arrest before it and reprimanded. But for having written a "discourteous and intemperate" letter to the Speaker and thus having been disrespectful to the House, he was held guilty of contempt of the Assembly for the second time and was sentenced to serve seven days' imprisonment in Lucknow District Jail. Keshav Singh filed a writ-petition before the Lucknow Bench of Allahabad High Court, praying for quashing the detention order on the ground that his detention after the reprimand was unconstitutional. The High Court, pending final decision ordered his release on bail. The Assembly strongly reacted and resolved that the two honourable judges of the High Court who had heard the case, together with petitioner Keshav Singh and his lawyer had committed breach of privilege of the House. Accordingly, warrants were issued against them by the Speaker. On a counterpetition filed by the two judges before the High Court, a Full Bench of 28 judges heard and stayed the processes of the Assembly until disposal of the case. Later, the Speaker referred the matter to the Privileges Committee, and as recommended by the committee, the warrants issued against the judges were withdrawn but the contemners were summoned to give explanation to the House, which the judges declined to respond to. To resolve the impasse, the President of India referred the matter to the Supreme Court for advice under Article 143 of the Constitution. A special bench of seven judges ruled by a six to one majority that 'the content of Article 194(3) must ultimately be determined by the courts and not by legislatures; that the writ jurisdiction of the High Court under Article 226 is not subject to privileges; that the fundamental right to move the Supreme Court for enforcement of fundamental rights, embodied in Article 32, is not subject to privileges; that the guarantee of personal liberty embodied in Article 21 applies when the legislatures exercise their powers in respect of their privileges; and that Article 22(1) exempts from judicial scrutiny only irregularities in legislative proceedings; but if the impugned procedure is illegal and unconstitutional, it would be open to judicial scrutiny by a court of law. Later the U.P. Assembly resolved that the opinion of the Supreme Court was wrong. In the Presidential Reference, the U.P. Assembly, though made appearance through lawyer, maintained that as under Article 143 the supreme Court was not exercising any judicial function, so they by no means were submitting to the jurisdiction of the court. The Supreme Court was pained to see the trend in the legislative bodies tenaciously refusing to acknowledge the jurisdiction of the courts over them, and raised the question : Was it the intention of the Constitution to perpetuate the dualism which rudely disturbed public life in England in the 17th, 18th and 19th centuries? In a recent Press interview, Kusum Kant Jain; the youngest signatory of the Constitution has reiterated that the founder-fathers created constitutional safeguard and if people try to 'molest' the Constitution by bending it to suit their needs, then there is a provision whereby the apex court can cancel them.

For complete one decade the confrontation gained its momentum and it ultimately culminated into a legislative attempt to undo the position settled by the Supreme Court, by substituting clause (3) of Article 194 by the 42nd Amendment to the Constitution, which dropped the reference to legislation to codify the privileges at any point of time or any reliance on the privileges of the British House of Commons, and provided that the privileges of each House of legislature "shall be such as may from time to time be evolved by such House." The amendment could not come into force, as, before issuance of the notification required to be issued under section 1 (2) of the 42nd Amendment Act, 1976 the government headed by Smt. Indira Gandhi fell and the Janata Dal government came to power. As a result, the pre-1976 text of Article 194 continued to occupy the field till it was amended in 1978 by the 44th Constitution Amendment Act. Under the law as amended by the 44th Amendment Act (i) the ultimate source of privileges continues to flow from legislation; and (ii) until such legislation is made, the pre-constitution law as upto April, 1979 will be the source of such privileges. Obviously the position relating to legislative privileges as held by the Supreme Court in the Reference case survived the 42nd Amendment of the Constitution, and when read with the 44th Amendment, it stands as follows : That according to the rule of harmonious construction, all parts of the Constitution when read together make the provisions relating to privileges subject to the Fundamental Rights and Art. 32 and 226; and that Arts. 20-21,

22(1) and 22(2) would be attracted to invalidate an order of the legislature for breach of privilege.

The 44th Amendment brought another important change in the law relating to privileges of state legislatures. Prior to 1976, the law relating to protection of publication of proceedings of legislatures was different as between the Union and the State legislatures. So far as the Parliament is concerned, it had enacted the Parliamentary Proceedings (Protection of Publication) Act, 1956; but so far as the state legislatures are concerned, they were not covered by that Central Act, nor the law made by themselves was uniform. There was no exemption from sec. 499 I.P.C. During the Emergency, the Central Government felt that high dignitaries should be given protection from defamatory publications in the Press, even though they related to reports of Parliament. Accordingly in 1976, first by an Ordinance and then by a Repealing Act, the Parliamentary Proceedings (Protection of Publication) Act, 1977 and also to give uniform coverage to the state legislatures. Art. 361-A was inserted by the 44th Constitution Amendment Act, 1978, with effect from 20th June, 1979. Therefore, the need for separate legislation for the state legislatures remained no longer there. Besides, the immunity under Art. 361-A would be available equally in relation to the Parliament and the state legislatures and in respect of civil as well as criminal proceeding or liability. Being a constitutional provision it would have overriding effect over section 499, I.P.C. it would protect a legislature against publication of its expunged reports or matters and from malicious publication or publication of garbled or perverted reports.

These measures, however, failed to stop the on-going confrontation between the judiciary and the legislature, even though the Supreme Court made it clear in 1970 in the case of Tej Kiran that the immunity available under Article 194(2) is complete and what the legislators would say in the House is subject to the rules of the legislature concerned, and subject to the control of proceedings by the Speaker; and that Courts have no say in the matter. But the courts again became sensitive when the conduct of some Judges was discussed in the Legislative Council of Karnataka during its session in 1978, which gave rise to the High Court case of Subbiah *vs.* Karnataka Legislative Council, which lays down that a court cannot send for proceedings of the legislature to determine whether any member of the legislature has violated Art. 211 by any words uttered by him in course of discussion in the House of which he is a member. The battle opened up greatly on another front, relating to the powers of the courts to inquire into proceedings of any legislature and the immunity from the jurisdiction of any court as provided in Article 212(2). Right in 1965, the year of the Presidential Reference mentioned earlier, the Supreme Court refused special leave to an appeal from the decision of the Punjab High Court rejecting a writ-petition of Madhu Limaye against the Speaker. The courts consistently upheld that though the immunity from judicial interference is confined to matters of irregularity of procedure, still, even an erroneous decision or interpretation of the Rules of legislative procedure by the Speaker cannot be subject-matter of scrutiny in a court of law. Neither the Supreme Court nor any High Court can act as a court of revision against the legislature or any rulings of the Speaker with respect to the proceedings within the House concerned. There had been a spate of cases in various High Courts on the related issues during the period from 1951 to 1965, while the arena remained almost empty for next fifteen years, the battle-line having been clearly drawn. There might have been one or two isolated incident, but on the whole the controversy subsided partly because of the Supreme Court's historical advice in 1965, partly because of the Court's due recognition of the parliamentary privileges and immunities to strike a balance and harmony in respective functioning, and partly because of the 42nd and 44th Constitution Amendment Acts which kept on guard both the judiciary and the legislature.

The unholy confrontation resurfaced in 1989 with much bitterness this time, when on 25th April, 1989 the Supreme Court by an interim order directed for provisional release of 32 Youth Congress workers who had been sentenced by the Andhra Pradesh Assembly Speaker to undergo 30 days' imprisonment for contempt of the House, on the fact that they had stormed the Assembly premises on 29th March while the Assembly had been in session.

By the time the state authorities received the order of the Supreme Court, the 32 detenues had already served 29 days' imprisonment. Despite this irony of the judicial process, the reaction from members of the Assembly, belonging to almost all parties and the Speaker in a significant ruling held that "the High Court or Supreme court cannot go into the question of corrections, propriety or any action taken in respect of the breach of privilege or contempt of the House." The Speaker further ruled that the Parliament and the State Legislatures, in their own right, are supreme and not subordinate to the judiciary. The higher courts cannot, in any petition under Article 226 or Article 32 of the Constitution sit in appeal over the decision of the Legislative Assembly. The legislature has its own procedure and it is the sole judge whether a contempt has been committed or not, according to the Speaker, G. Narayana Rao. In a seething attack, the Speaker indicated the Supreme Court judges for showing "haste" and "casualness" in their action, and by a 'warrant of commitment' directed the Police Commissioner of Hyderabad to re-arrest them to serve the remaining one day's imprisonment. In turn, a five-judge bench of the Supreme Court issued a notice to the Speaker to show cause why a contempt proceeding should not be initiated against him, for his act constituting *prima facie* disobedience of the Court's order. Legal experts and the Press at large took side with the Supreme Court on the issue, viewing that Judges of the Supreme Court having no powers of their, they rather are the trusted custodians of the rights of the citizens, with unlimited powers to interpret and administer the Constitution as they find it. No other authority can review it. "One visible good resulted from the tussle is that the members of the House made a strong demand to codify the privileges, perhaps for the first time".

Within a few years, the Maharashtra Assembly intended to summon a High Court judge for an alleged breach of privilege. When the eminent jurist, Mr. Nani Palkhivala, protested against this kind an article, some members of the legislature demanded his arrest. Most of the Bar Association condemned the matter which ultimately ended in confusion.

Perhaps the most enigmatic case was the controversy which

arose in between the Manipur Assembly Speaker, Mr. Borobabu Singh, and the Supreme Court some time back. Initially it was not a case relating to any Legislative Privilege or powers of the Speaker or his subjugation to the Supreme Court's jurisdiction. Rather the case related to the speaker's role and function in his capacity as the administrative head of the Assembly Secretariat concerned. Still the entire issue assumed an unholy shape of battle over subtle supremacy and resulted in a country-wide campaign against Judicial activism viewed as "judicial excesses" from some corners. In fact, it was a constructive endeavour on the part of the Supreme Court to point to the fact that over the last many years, the legislatures in India had little or no time to take a critical look at their own Secretariat meant to serve their legislation duties. Due to legislative concerns and impartial secretariat advice were not adequately reflected in the day-to-day business. Effective functioning of any legislature largely depends on the efficiency and expertise of its officers comprising the Secretariat. In spite of a well-considered view reflected in the Report on Parliament Secretariat that as a general rule, direct recruitment to such secretariats should be resorted to only in the cases where the persons within the secretariat are not found suitable either on the grounds of the required qualifications and ability for the specific job or work and conduct, the secretariats in the Parliament as well as in the State Legislatures are being oftener filled up with officials from other services, whose ignorance of the complex functioning and dynamics of legislature only complicates things for the worse. In the normal course such officers would not have found a place if the Presiding officers of the legislatures concerned stuck to the age old conventions and rules as laid out from time to time. They contribute to a large extent for such confrontations and for malfunctioning of the legislature in India, it is said.

The conflict, may it be of power, or supremacy or jurisdiction, continues and this time with the Delhi legislature and the Delhi High Court, while the common people usually remain unconcerned, coming back to the scene in Mizoram, one recalls that the first move by the Assembly to claim, assert, and protest against the breach of its privileges was made on 29th March, 1973 when a notice was received from Mr. Saitlawma an MLA against the Editor, Printer and Publisher of HMAR ARSI, a local Mizo Daily, alleged to have cast reflection on the chair and lowered the dignity of the House for publishing a news item in its issue of 27th March, 1973. The news item read as follows : "Due to late coming of the Speaker by five minutes, the Assembly resumed its sitting at 10-05 yesterday.....In the afternoon members could only have budget discussion at 2043. Whether it was due to Speaker's ignorance of rules, allotment of time to each member was announced after 8 minutes". The committee of Privileges headed by Mr. Hiphei, then Deputy Speaker made its report on 27.6.73 by recommending to accept the apology tendered by the newspaper editor and impressing upon that : "The press plays an important role in Parliamentary Democracy. The press is the standard vehicle for the dissemination of public opinion.... If there be no mutual respect between the legislature and the press, then democracy cannot thrive". This might be one of the most ideal and rational approaches of any legislature to such issue.

The conflict, may it be of power, or supremacy or jurisdiction, continues and this time with the Delhi legislature and the Delhi High Court, while the common people usually remain unconcerned, unmoved and perhaps disillusioned, majority of the common people do not possess the wisdom to read between the lines and truly understand the scholastic and bulky judgments even when passed to their benefits. Many more are ignorant of the parliamentary privileges. A study was revealed that parliamentary privileges are unknown to 41 countries which have adopted the Westminster Parliamentary system, as this has not been detrimental to the functioning of the popular representatives. On the other hand, a Time MODE poll conducted in nine metropolitan cities during last week of February 1996 shows that a large majority of common people, almost 78 per cent, endorsed judicial activism and held it justified. Many of the common people strongly feel that one indisputable good of judicial activism has been an enhanced public awareness of rights. There was a near consensus on judicial activism at a symposium held at New Delhi on 12th January, 1997, holding that it had helped bring order and that "it was need of the hour," though legal experts many a times differ on correctness and limits of judicial activism. The former Chief Justice of India, Justice Y.V. Chandrachud while delivering Asutosh Memorial Lecture on 26.6.94 emphasized the need of codifying the powers and privileges of the legislature and traced the cause of the growing tension between the legislature and the judiciary, as the politicians were keen to frame laws that might boost their popularity, even though 'unconstitutional'. However, he strongly justified the judicial activism in no unclear or ambiguous terms. In a society bereft of ethics and values, he said, the Supreme Court must transcend the limitation of law to be of any use to the society for which laws are framed. Sometime in December, 1995, the eminent jurist who though suffered the brunt of the legislature for alleged breach of legislative privilege, admitted that the Supreme Court as well as the 18 High Courts are vested with the widest possible powers given by any Constitution in the world. But even then, according to him they are not expected to decide, and should never decide, questions of political wisdom or public policy. It is not for the courts to function as an extended and of the executive. Justice M.N. Venkatachalaiah who had probably set the tone for judicial activism as thc Chief Justice of India supported the role of the judiciary on the grounds that a federal Constitution which sustains and survives on the spirit of the balance amongst thc various branches of government makes the judiciary an arbiter of the limits of powers as also the limits of the extent of the powers of the legislative and executive wings. It may be appropriate to recall what Pandit Nehru said at the time of shaping the Constitution :

> "You may say that there is no assurance that the Judges will interpret the mores of their day more wisely and truly than other men. I am not disposed to deny this, but in my view it is quite beside the point. The point is rather that this power of interpretation must be lodged somewhere, and the custom of the constitution has lodged it in the Judges, if they are to fulfil their functions as Judges, it could hardly be lodged elsewhere.

Their conclusions must, indeed, be subject to constant testing, retesting, revision, and adjustment; but if they act with conscience and intelligence, they aught to attain in their conclusions a fair average of truth and wisdom."

This may be the answer to the controversy. May not be a full-stop, but at least as a semi-colon; And to conclude, one may recall, the judiciary's humble claim to define itself with all humility, as Justice Jackson of the U.S. Supreme Court said on behalf of the entire judiciary : "We are not final because we are infallible, but we are infallible because we are final."

SELECTED READINGS

Basu, Durga Das, *Shorter Constitution of India*, 11th Edition : Prentice Hall of India Private Ltd., New Delhi.

Hidayatulla, M., – *Miscellanea* : N.M. Tripathi Private Ltd. Bombay, 1988

Mizoram Gazette, 1973.

Statesman dt. 26/11/1965.

Statesman dt. 15/12/96.

Statesman dt. 9/1/97.

Statesman dt. 13/1/97.

Telegraph dt. 15/9/89.

Telegraph dt. 3/10/89.

Telegraph dt. 20/3/93.

Telegraph dt. 11/11/93.

Telegraph dt. 20/11/93.

Telegraph dt. 20/1/94.

Telegraph dt. 26/1/94.

Telegraph dt. 6/4/94.

Telegraph dt. 13/6/94.

Telegraph dt. 27/6/94.

Telegraph dt. 1/11/95.

Telegraph dt. 3/3/96.

Telegraph dt. 28/12/96.

Telegraph dt.7/1/97.

Times of India dt. 28/9/89.

Times of India dt. 7/10/89.

Times of India dt. 23/5/92.

Times of India dt. 4/12/95.

Times of India dt. 5/3/96.

Times of India dt. 17/7/96.

Times of India dt. 22/7/96.

Times of India dt. 2/12/96.

Times of India dt. 4/12/96.

Times of India dt. 6/1/97.

Times of India dt. 13/1/97.

14

REVIEW OF THE INDIAN CONSTITUTION

The President K.R. Narayanan's address on February 23, 2000 to the joint session of Parliament makes the point succinctly: Complementing the Constitution by stating that it has "Served Well", the President K.R. Narayanan said, it had been a reliable guarantor of Parliamentary democracy, secularism and fundamental rights which all of us cherish. The Constitution has also inspired the spread of democratic consciousness in our society, empowering *Dalits, Adivasis*, backward classes and women, making our system of governance more participative and progressive".

At the special function in Parliament Central Hall to celebrate 50 years of the Indian Constitution, the Prime Minister, Atal Behari Vajpayee, stressed upon the need for a Commission to review the Constitution for the purpose of political stability, the people's impatience for faster development and removal of regional and social imbalances. On the same platform, the President K.R. Narayanan noted :

> Our recent experience of instability in government is perhaps not sufficient reason to discard the Parliamentary system in favour of the Presidential or any other system.

He further said :

> "Today we have to consider whether it is the Constitution that has failed us or whether it is we, who have failed the Constitution."

He further added very relevantly :

We should not blame the Constitution for the ills that affect us or for our failures, shortcomings and no review panel can recommend tinkering with the basic features of our Constitution. No review as is, thus obvious, can afford to alter or destroy the basic structures of the Constitution. In various historic judgements, the Supreme Court has identified rule of law, judicial review, parliamentary democracy, federalism and secularism as the basic features of the Indian Constitution which cannot be altered. The law is very clear in the light of the rulings in Kesavananda Bharati *versus* State of Kerala, (1973) wherein the Supreme Court held that while the Parliament has the power to amend any part of the Constitution, it cannot amend/alter or destroy the basic features of the Constitution. As such, the basic features must be retained.

The Preamble Provisions, the Fundamental Rights and the Directive Principles of State Policy are also the basic principles of the Constitution, though, some of the provisions are amendable like any other part of the Constitution.

Thus, the basic structures of the Constitution must remain the same. But there are some grey areas/aspects that can be looked into keeping in mind the overall welfare of the people :

1. The word "Socialist" in the Preamble of the Constitution is vague and irrelevant. India has never been a socialist state. The Indian liberal democratic political system has been building up a capitalist oriented society instead of socialist since Independence which gives rise to social, political and economic conflicts/tensions. The New Economic Policy (liberalisation, privatisation and globalisation – market, friendly, economy) contradicts socialist and other preamble provisions. Socialist provision, thus, needs to be reviewed.

2. **Part III containing Fundamental Rights**

(a) An egalitarian educational structure, making effective provision to ensure Right to Education in Part III of the Constitution has to be made. Education is both means as well as the end result of development. It is the basic needs of the people and their human rights. It is the most powerful instrument for the empowerment of the people. Right to education has also been held to be a fundamental right by the Supreme Court.

(b) The Right to Work without which Article 21 would remain a pious wish, needs to be included. The Supreme Court has interpreted the *right to life* which implies *the right to livelihood* and more than that the *right to residence* proximate to the place of work. The Supreme Court, thus, mentions Article 21 to include the *right to livelihood and shelter/residence.* To create more jobs to tackle both poverty and unemployment is a need to make these rights meaningful. Unemployment/ poverty is an economic malady and a social curse. Both degrade man, generate hatred, depress social activities and economic prosperity and constitute a great social liability to social stability. In such context, to talk of development, ignoring any reference to unemployment and poverty is hypocritical. But it is also true that the western development model and new package of economic policies have a jobless growth and cannot aleviate poverty and eradicate unemployment unless there is restructuring the existing model of development on capitalist lines and socio-economic power structure. Both questions are power questions rooted in the development model.

(c) The Right to Information for ensuring efficient, responsive, open, transparent, accessible and accountable of the democratic governance needs to be included in the Chapter III of the Constitution.

3. Part IV containing the Directive Principles of State Policy

Directive Principles of State Policy under Article 37 is non-justiciable or non-enforceable by any court, no doubt but the principles are fundamental in the governance of the country and it shall be the duty of the state to apply these principles in making laws. In the end, the liberal democratic political system of India has *in toto* failed to translate these objectives into practice/reality owing to their bring non-justiciable and also the adoption of the capitalist model of modernisation since Independence and thereby unachieved social, political and economic justice.

The adoption of the new economic and financial reforms (Liberalisation, Privatisation and Globalisation) since 1991 by the liberal democratic state of India violates or offends the Directive Principles, vulgarising our lower middle class and brutalising our disadvantaged, vulnerable/lower poor class. For instance, the report of the ILU-Asian Region Team for Employment, Promotion entitled India: Employment and Economic Policies, December 1993. The findings are that both underemployment and open employment increased since the new package of policies from 1991 that there had been a fall in real wages for casual labour in both urban and rural areas and that the incidence of poverty had increased both in urban and rural areas and also steep increase in food prices by over 45 per cent in three years between 1989-90 and 1992-93.

4. The spectre of the New Labour Policy – Golden Shake Hand/ exit policy has been haunting/hitting the working people since the adoption of the new package of policies which contradicts Article 43 of the Directive Principles. So, there has to be wide diffusion of ownership and control of material resources of the community and prevention of concentration of wealth and means of production to the common detriment. Policies, which may promote income inequality, inegalitarianism in asset holding, concentration of economic power would certainly go against the spirit, if not the letter of the Directive Principles of State Policy. Briefly, the danger or an adverse impact of the new package of policies is evident all around.

(a) It is, therefore, suggested that the promises and good intentions articulated in Article-39 (A,B,C,E and F) 43, 45 and 47 and other humane provisions of the Directive Principles of State Policy of the Constitution have to be given the status of legally enforceable fundamental rights for the purpose of sustained and continuous uplift of the socio-economic conditions of the life of the deprived/vulnerable/exploited sections of the Indian society.

(b) However, there is a need to insert provisicns for political parties which shed communalism and consensual democracy in the country encompassing several identities. Communalism is subversive of our political stability, secularism and socio-economic development. The framers of the Constitution overlooked this need.

(c) There is talk of political instability and also the recommendation of the only other system more stable—the presidential system. Any system of democratic government survives on twin principles of accountability and stability. Ambedkar had underlined these two principles in the Constituent Assembly and had emphasised accountability over stability. In the absence of a strong and responsible party system, even stability may prove to be a mirage. In fact as an alternative to systematic change, the German practice of constructive vote of non-confidence has been proposed. This system entails that alongwith expressing non-confidence in a Prime Minister, the House proposes an alternative leader. Unless the House elects an alternative leader, the vote of non-confidence is not carried. This system has the same danger as the executive Presidency. It strengthens the Prime Minister, as the German Chancellor has been strengthened. It would give stability at the cost of accountability. Consider a bad Prime Minister not being able to be removed even by his party for lack of an alternative. Further, would this system be introduced only at the Centre? How is going to be reconciled in the context of Centre-State relations in the state?

(d) Article 105 and 194 provide that the Parliament by law can codify the privileges of the Parliament. Till date, no step in this direction has been taken. The Constitution must provide a Code of Ethics for the legislators and for this purpose, Articles 105 and 194 must be amended. The Supreme Court has now taken this power.

(e) Dcfection is itself undemocratic, encouraging and legitimising unparliamentary voting behaviour and splits in the party. There should be simple provision that if an M.P. and M.L.A. elected on one party's ticket, joins another political party, her/his seat would automatically stand vacated. However, there should be no disqualification attached to disobedience to the party whip, excepting in a vote of confidence, or a vote of no confidence or voting on a money bill. In all other cases, the member's right of free speech and voting should be maintained.

(f) The Legislative Councils (Upper House) in many states are needless financial burden and serve only the purpose of providing for political favours. These should be abolished.

(g) The Parliament, along time back, had passed a resolution suggesting amending the Constitution so, that the maximum strength of the Council of Ministers should not be more than 10 per cent of the members of the Lok Sabha and one per cent of Rajya Sabha. The same provision was also to be applied to the state. For this purpose, the Constitution needs to be amended.

(h) In the states, legislators are appointed Chairmen of Public Sector units. This leads to nepotism and inefficiency and must be prohibited.

(i) To the constitutional provisions interpreted by Supreme Court, the Prime Minister can even be a member of the Rajya Sabha. To me, in all democracies, the Prime Minister is by convention and practice, a member of the House of the People. For India– the biggest democracy – the position cannot be otherwise.

5. Electoral Reforms

Success of democracy depends on free and fair elections. In order to have free and fair elections, a consideration of strengthening the Election Commission with more powers and its own cadre of officers to man its key offices in the state, the partial list system as prevalent in Germany – with a knowledge of certain difficulties in operationalising this in the Indian context; state funding of elections for the recognised national and state parties and their candidates as justified by the Inderjit Gupta Committee; compulsory voting law; auditing of the accounts of political parties; and rules for ensuring inner-party democracy in political parties are measures that do not require constitutional changes. These measures will also go a long way in ensuring political reforms necessary for a healthier political life in the country.

6. Review of Federal Structure/Fiscal Federalism/Autonomy/ Responsibility

To construct a new federal balance in India, the present centralised federation may be changed into a co-operative and constructive federal polity. Four measures are suggested :

(a) Territorial reorganisation of states on the basis of their being socio-culturally homogeneous and administratively and politically manageable. Economic viability to an extent also needs to be looked into.

(b) Amendment to the Constitution of greater administrative and fiscal powers to the states for effective socio-economic development and poiitical stability. Presently, the Finance Commission has made the balanced distribution of national resources between the union and the states; yet, it is has led to fiscal indiscipline by the states as regards public spending. Legislative control over the public finance/money is called for. The Vice-President Shri Krishna Kant reminded that "it is the legislature's duty in democracy to ensure that tax payer's money is spent for the purpose mentioned so that he benefits when there is development. The legislature should ensure that money is spent prudently because of the enormity of public expenditure– interest payment, subsidies and non-plan grants to some states along with other expenses account for 95 per cent of non-plan expenditure and 70 per cent of the total expenditure". The total government expending in the country is 33 per cent of G.D.P. The huge deficits in budget after budget are assaults on national savings rate, reducing overall aggregate investment that challenges the sustainability of high growth. In order to better fiscal management and to ensure financial discipline, Articles 292 and 293 need to be amended to make it mandatory for the Parliament to place constitutional limits on the borrowing powers of the government.

Besides, the Finance Commission needs to be strengthened making it a permanent by amending Article 280 of the Constitution. It should be renamed as Federal Finance Commission with two separate cells – Planning and Finance.

Fiscal federalism further needs to be reviewed from the perspective of the emerging third tier Panchayati Raj and Nagarpalika. Most states have not yet institutionalised the Third tier. The Constitution of the State Election Commission and State Finance Commission has a long way to go. The subjects in 11th and 12th schedules for the Third tier give them more responsibility than political power or independent fiscal resources. For this purpose, the whole gamut of inter-governmental relations has to be reviewed.

(c) The area that requires, is multi-level governance in the country. Activisation of the Panchayati Raj and Nagarpalika systems with necessary devolution to build active grassroot democracy by implementing the constitutional Seventy Third and Seventy Fourth Amendment Acts, relating to PRIs and Nagarpalika is emphasised. Now, it is the responsibility of the constitutional machineries to work the system uniformly throughout the country by amending parts IX and IXA, Articles 243 M to 243 ZG. of the Constitution.

(d) Building of a new federal consensus between parties, social activist groups, and citizens to fight communalism, casteism and separatism and to defend the values of democracy, secular polity, federal nation-building and social justice.

7. Governor and Article 356

There are two roughest edges in centre-state relations i.e. the role of Governor and Article 356. Article 356 has been used/misused more than 100 times in the last 50 years and very often for political reasons and not for the question of constitutional propriety or situation by all political parties in power. There is a need to rethink of the office and role of the Governor, when the basic features to the Constitution, its democratic and federal character are undermined by the decisions of the Council of Ministers.

(i) The President should not exclusively rely on the Governor's report rather he should obtain information through his independent and reliable sources. His decision to proclaim President's rule should depend on his satisfaction based on objective consideration.
(ii) The Governor should not have the power to report directly to the President on the issue of the constitutional break-down in a state. The power should be given to the Inter State Council or the North-Eastern Council (in case of the north-eastern states) as official bodies which may look into the reports on the state provided by the various heads of the State administration. The Inter-State Council or the North-Eastern Council if it is so satisfied, can bring the matter to the notice of the President about the prevailing situation in the state. The President may take decision on the Inter-State Council's report or the NEC's report to invoke Article 356.
(iii) The President should only dismiss the State Government and hold in abeyance the decision to dissolve the Assembly or place it under suspended animation and as such, a decision about the fate of legislature should await the approval of the relevant proclamation by Parliament with-two-thirds majority.

The Governor should remain above contreversy so that he can discharge his functions impartially and fearlessly. In view of the above, the suggestions relating to the appointment of the Governor below may be considered.

(i) A Committee comprising the Vice-President of India, the Prime Minister, the leader of the opposition and the Chief Justice of India should suggest the names to be appointed as the Governor of a State.
(ii) The Chief Minister of the state should be consulted by the President about the appointment of the Governor.

(iii) Persons of calibre, competence, integrity/character should be suggested for appointment as the Governor.

(iv) The recommendations of the Sarkaria Commission regarding the appointment of Governor may be seriously looked into which would help in appointing non-controversial persons as Governors.

Extreme suggestions have been also made by some academic jurists that both the office of the Governor and Aritcle 356 should be abolished/deleted. As a result, the country will save more than hundred crores of rupees spent annually on ornamental luxury in the maintenance and sustenance of this institutional adifice.

8. Judicial System : Reform

Collapsing of Judicial system in which obtaining of justice has become too difficult, expensive for the poor, ever delayed and frustrating. The judicial system has no simple and speedy procedures. It needs to be reformed. Regarding the appointment of judges, more knowledge of Civil or Criminal law should not be the only consideration, for in the course of their function judges have to decide vital issues relating to human rights of the disadvantaged/deprived, the conflict between globalisation and rural economy and gender justice. So, the power of the appointment, transfer and discipline of judges should be given to the National Judicial Commission consisting of the Executive and the Judiciary, of course retaining the primary of the latter.

There is no uniformity in the retirement of the judges (judge of subordinate court at 60, High Court 62 and Supreme Court 65 years). The lack of uniformity in the retirement age of judges would difinitely affect the judicial Independence. Article 124(7) needs to be amended.

9. Socio-Economic Transformation and Eradication of Poverty and Unemployment/Implementation of Land Reforms

The adoption of new economic policy of the Government (liberalisation, privatisation and globalisation) and the existing socio-economic power structure affect the socio-economic development of the Indian masses especially the poor. Eradication of poverty and unemployment depends on the restructuring of the existing socio-economic order, based on capitalist/western model of deve-lopment, human relationships, new package of policies, and state intervention and not on the retreating state. Briefly, the western/capitalist development model and new package of policies have a jobless growth and cannot alleviate poverty. These need a fresh look.

State led development and community based participative development instead of market led development are emphasised. Markets are not the natural friends of people; they have to be made people friendly through government intervention. The state must not withdraw from the basic responsibilities of social welfare towards the deprived and the vulnerable and infrastructure, nor unregulated foreign investment be allowed to cause social disruption. Foreign investment in consumer sectors has to be discouraged.

Besides, re-invigoration of economic growth with equitable distribution of wealth and social justice is to be emphasised/ considered. People contribute to be growth and growth contribute to the people's well-being. State regulated market and market regulated enterprise should be a goal of this country.

Implementation of genuine and effective land reforms and ceiling acts all over the country and restructuring the land lord and landless relationships has to be made. After all, in India a country of village, land is the most dominant aspect in the rural power structure. If the land is distributed to the weaker sections and women, they would be better placed to play a meaningful role in rural affairs. This also increases domestic market opportunities.

Amartya Sen has also suggested that if India can spend more resources on education, health and implement land reforms, democratic strength of India can be restored.

What is lacking is the political will for consensual democracy in which all marginalised communities get due share in governance. Political stability can be achieved through sacular governments, power sharing (Federal balance), and consensus and strengthening civil society.

However, any machine is as good as the person operating it. It is unfortunate that like bad workmen, our politicians are blaming the tools, tools that they have designed and operated for a half a century. No Constitution can work successfully without a spirit of constitutionalism. Constitutionalism, understood as a process of democratic and participative governance, is also an instrument of reducing partisanship in decision-making. The question is that the Constitution may be reformed, but would it instil the spirit of Constitutionalism in our political class?

SELECT READINGS

Administrative Review : An Annual Journal of Indian Institute of Public Administration, Mizoram Regional Branch, Aizawal, (1996-97-Issues).

Bakshi, P.M. *The Constitution of India : With Selective Comments*, New Delhi, Universal Law Publishing Company, 2000 (Reprint).

Economic and Political Weekly, Mumbai (All Issues from January 2000 to September 2000).

Mainstream (Weekly), New Delhi (All Issues of 1999 to September 2000).

Prasad, R.N., Emerging Challenges of the Governance of India (Unpublished).

Politics India, New Delhi, (All Issues of 1999 upto September 2000).

Saha, Tushar Kanti, Reviewing the Working of the Indian Constitution, (Theme paper for Annual Member's Conference of IIPA- 1999-2000, New Delhi (unpublished).

Times of India, Hindustan Times, Hindu and *Statesman* (National Dailies only concerning the issues/articles of Reviewing the Constitution of India.

BIBLIOGRAPHY

Abdul Aziz and David D. Arnold, (eds.), *Decentralised Governance in Asian Countries*, New Delhi, Sage, 1996.

Alatas, Syed Hussein, *Corruption: Its Nature, Causes and Functions*, Aldershot: Avebury, 1990.

Anand, D.A., *Electoral Reforms : Curbing Role of Money Power*, New Delhi, IIPA, 1990.

Andhyarujina, T.R., *Judicial Activism and Constitutional Democracy in India*, Bombay : N.M. Tripathi, 1992.

Arora, Ramesh K., *People's Participation in Development Process*, Jaipur: HCMRIPA, 1979.

Banerjee, Ajit M. and K.A. Chandrasekaran, *Renewing Governance : Issues and Options*, New Delhi, McGraw Hill, 1996.

Basu, Debashis and Suchetaz Dalal, *The Scam : Who Won Who Lost Who Got Away*, New Delhi, IMS, 1993.

Baxi Upendra, *On Judicial Activism, Legal Education, and Research in a Globalising India*, New Delhi, Capital Foundation Society, 1996.

Bhambhri, C.P., *Bureaucracy and Politics in India*, Delhi, Vikas, 1971.

Bhattacharya, Mohit, *Restructuring Public Administration: Essays in Rehabilitation*, New Delhi, Jawahar, 1997.

Chatterjee, Partha, (ed.), *State and Politics in India*, Delhi, Oxford University Press, 1997.

Chaturvedi, V.N., (ed.), *Quest for Commitment in Public Service*, New Delhi, Department of Personnel and Administrative Reforms, 1975.

Chaturvedi, T.N., (ed.), *Ethics in Public Life*, New Delhi, IIPA, 1996.

Chaturvedi, T.N., (ed.), *Contemporary Administrative Culture of India*, New Delhi, IIPA, 1996.

Chopra, S.K., (ed.), *Towards Good Governance*, Delhi, Konark, 1997.

Clarke, Michael, *Corruption : Causes, Consequences and Control*, London : Frances Printer (Publishers), 1983.

Damodaran, K.M., *Accountability in Administration – Case for Employees Charter*, New Delhi, IIPA, 1998.

Das Gupta, Monica; Lincoln C. and T.N., Krishnan (eds.), *Health, Poverty and Development in India*, Delhi, Oxford University Press, 1996.

Demko, G.J., *Population Geography: A Reader*, New York, McGraw Hill, 1970.

Desai, Meghnad and Paul Redfern (eds.), *Global Governance: Ethics and Economics of the World Order*, London : Pinter, 1995.

Dodd, Lawrence C., *Coalitions in Parliamentary Government*, New Jersey : Princeton University Press, 1976.

Dwivedi, Onkar P.; R.B. Jain and Dhirendra K. Vajpei (eds.), *Governing India : Issues concerning Public Policy*, Institutions and Administration, Delhi, B.R. Publishing, 1998.

Girling, John, *Corruption, Capitalism and Democracy*, London : Routledge, 1997.

Haque, M. Samsul, *Restructuring Development Theories and Policies : A Critical Study*, Albany, N.Y., State University of New York Press, 1999.

Hanumantha Rao, C.H. and Hans Linnemann, (eds.), *Economic Reforms and Poverty Alleviation in India*, New Delhi, Sage, 1996.

Heywood, Paul, (ed.), *Political Corruption*, Oxford : Black Well, 1997.

Hirst, Paul and Grahame Thompson, *Glabalisation in Question : The International Economy and the Possibilities of Governance*, Cambridge : Polity Press, 1996.

Kashyap, Subhash C., *Coalition Government and Politics in India*, New Delhi, Uppal, 1997.

Kashyap, Subhas, C., (ed.), *Crime and Corruption to Good Governance*, New Delhi, Uppal, 1997.

Kohli, Atul, *Democracy and Discontent India's Growing Crisis of Government*, Cambridge : Cambridge University Press, 1991.

Kothari Rajni, *State against Democracy : In Search of Humane Governance*, New Delhi, Ajanta, 1989.

Kausar, J. Azam, (ed.), *Federalism and Good Governance : Issues across Cultures*, New Delhi, South Asian, 1998.

Levi, Michael and David Malken (eds.), *The Corruption of Politics and the Politics of Corruption*, Oxford : Black Well, 1996.

Lewis, John P., *India's Political Economy : Governance and Reform*, Delhi, Oxford University Press, 1995.

Mansukhani, H.C., *Corruption and Public Servants*, New Delhi, Vikas, 1979.

Mathur, Kuldeep, *Development Policy and Administration*, New Delhi, Sage, 1996.

Mehta, Jaswant B., *Quest For a Better Democratic Alternative*, Bombay : Forum For Better Democratic Alternative, 1995.

Mishra, Sweta, *Democratic Decentralisation in India : Study in Retrospect and Prospect*, New Delhi, Mittal, 1994.

Mitra ,A., *India's Population : Aspects of Quality and Control*, Vol. II, New Delhi, 1978.

Mitra, Chandan, *The Corrupt Society*, New Delhi, Penguin India, 1998.

Muriekan, J., *Poverty in India : Challenges and Responses*, Trivandrum : A Xavier Board Publication, 1988.

Pai Panandiker, V.A. and Ajay K. Mehta, *The Indian Cabinet : A Study in Governance*, New Delhi, Konark, 1996.

Papola, T.S., *Anti-Poverty and Special Employment Programme in India : Their Role and Effectiveness under the Structural Adjustment Programme*, Washington: D.C., World Bank, 1993.

Ravi Prakash, *Constitution, Fundamental Rights, and Judicial Activism in India*, Jaipur, Mangal Deep Publication, 1997.

Saxena, Pradeep K., *Modern Governance*, Jaipur, RBSA Publishers, 1995.

Sen Gupta, Bhabani, *India : Problems of Governance*, Delhi, Konark, 1996.

Sinha, Ajit Kumar, (ed.), *New Economic Policy of India : Restructuring and Liberalising the Economy for 21st Century*, New Delhi, Deep and Deep, 1994.

Tummala, K.K., *Public Administration in India*, Delhi, Allied, 1996.

Turner, Mark and David Hulme, Governance, Administration and Development : Making the State Work, London: Mac Millan Press, 1997.

Wardm Peter M. (ed.), *Corruption, Development and Inequality : Soft Touch or Hard Graft*, London, Routledge, 1989.

INDEX

Accountability, 19, 25, 37, 41, 58, 94, 108, 211

Adivasis, 207

Administrative challenge, 35-36
- goals for, 107-108
- system, 15

Agricultural production, 32

Agricultural reforms, 103

AIADMK, 185

Alan Beals, 176

Anti-poverty programmes, budget allocation of, 22

Autonomy, 166

Bangladesh, 56

Below poverty line, 57

Bhambhri, C. P., 39

Bhattacharya, Mohit, 39

Bharatiya Janata Party (BJP), 67, 68

Big business houses, 14, 29

BJP-led coalition, 185

BJP-led Government, 186-187

Black marketers, 37

Black money, 28

Blunt, E., 175

Bodo's movement, 150

Bureaucracy, 15, 28, 39, 40-41
- politicisation of, 37

Capitalism, 14,15, 35, 162

Capitalist, 46
- classes, 14
- model, 57
- path, 84

Caste groups, 45, 83

Caste politicisation, 177, 180

Caste war, 147

Centralised federation, 53

Chakmas, 148

Challenges, 18-20, 26, 29, 55, 156, 159, 161

Chandrachud, Y. V. (Justice), 204

Chandrashekhar, 69

Child labour, 21

Child Labour Regulation and Abolition Act, 130

Civic governance, 16

Civil disobedience movement, 152

Coalition, 23
- formation, 64
- longevity, 64
- partners agreement, 69

Coalition politics, model of, 67
- system, 69, 72

Coalition Government, 180, 187
- common programmes, 75
- factor of, 65
- prospects of, 63, 75
  - observations/suggestions, 68, 70
- stability, of, 74

Communal riots, 37, 58, 60, 84
- sensitive issues of, 61

Communalism, 66, 84-85, 86-87, 88, 211

Conflicts, 43, 53, 60, 149-150

Congress coalition, 26

Congress Party, 63-64, 67-68

Constitution of India, 17, 20, 30, 44-45, 47, 49-50, 52, 60, 65, 80-81, 84, 145, 176

Constitutional objectives, 13

Constitutionalism, 17, 43, 44, 46, 61

Constraints, 124

Contradictions, 96, 97, 146

Corrupt election system, 57

Corruption, 28, 33, 37, 38, 40, 57, 100, 108, 151

Corruption free administration, 158

Criminalisations, 27, 37, 108, 116
- politics, 57

Crippled political development, 28

Crisis, 19, 54

Dahl, Robert, 141
Dalits, 207
Decentralised planning, 87, 92
Decentralisation, 14, 17
Decision-making, 111-114
Democracy, 89, 168
    quintessence of, 74
Democratic constitutional, goals of, 100
Democratic decentralisation, 20, 57, 102, 128
Democratic governance, 26
    legitimacy, 19, 25, 179
    participation, 14, 18, 23
    socialist arrangement, 62, 161
    system, 144
Democratisation, 85
Deprivation, 84-85, 100
Deve Gowda, H. D., 68, 69, 76
Diamont, Alfred, 180
Dichotomies, 142
Dictatorship, 65
Directive Principles of State Policy, 176, 178, 209-210
Discrimination, 14, 20, 81-82
    prohibition of, 49
Disintegration, process of, 26
Disparities, 47, 49, 100, 165
Dissolution of House, 74
Distributive justice, 62, 161
Divorce, 83
Drinking water, 33

Economic challenges, 19
Economic crisis, 29-30
Economic development, 167
Economic empowerment, 97, 119, 137
Economic governance, 16
Economic growth re-invigoration of, 126-127, 156
Economic inequality, 85
Economic justice, 29-30, 31, 47-48
Economic reformers 102
Education, 49, 157, 166, 170
Educational institution, 81-82
Educational opportunities, 172
    policy, 88
    process, 171
    system, 20, 52, 86-87
Election, 186, 188
Election Commission, 27, 187
Election laws, 40, 108
Electoral politics, 181
Electoral reforms, 118, 212-13
Emergency, 199
    powers, 54, 56
    proclamation, 48
    rule, 187
Emerging challenges, 15
Employment, 39, 81, 154-155
    opportunities, 56
    schemes, 105
Employment exchanges, 33
Ethnic conflicts, 148-149
Exploitation, 85, 90, 100, 110
Exports, 103
Exports-Imports Policy (Exim Policy), 126

Farmers suicides, 32
Federal arrangement, 23
Federal structure, review of, 213
Federalism, 17, 53
    distortions of, 26
Finance Commission, 93
Financial reforms, 210
Fiscal federalism, 213-214
Food security, 21, 128
Foodgrain production, 32
Foreign investment, 102
Fourth general elections 1967, 63
Freedom of speech/expression, 166
Frustration, 36, 100, 122
Fundamental Rights, 143, 208-209
    provision of, 80, 87

GATT agreement, 48, 50, 99
George Fernandes, 37
*Gheraos,*51, 59, 152
Globalisation, 18, 31, 34, 36, 38, 60, 124-125, 126, 129, 138-139, 151, 155, 162

Good governance, fundamental of, 31
Governor, appointment of, 214-216
Governance performance, 17-18
Gram Panchayat, 92
Gross National Product (GNP), 165
Gujaral, I. K., 33

Hackman, G. G., 78
Hajongs, 148
Hartals, 51, 59
Hidayatullah, M. (Justice), 191, 193, 194
Higher education, 167, 169-170
House of Commons, 195, 197
Human development model, 15
Human freedom, 168-169
Human Freedom Index (HFI), 140
Human Rights Protection Commission, 109
Humane governance, 15-16
Hung Parliament, 75

Illiteracy, 20-21, 52, 169
Indian political system, 27
 aberrations in, 83
 achievement, 183
 structural contradictions, 46-47
Indira Gandhi, 55, 198
Indrajit Gupta Committee, 212
Industrial production, 32
Industrialisation, 66, 101
Intellectual property rights, 34
Inter-ethnic conflicts/violence, 148-149
Internal communal riots conflicts, 147-148
Internal disturbances/disorders, 60
Internal security 141, 160
 implications of, 59-60
 problems, 57
International Monetary Fund, (IMF), 55, 129, 137

Janata Dal, 67, 72, 185, 198
Janata Dal-led National front Government, 186
Janata Party, 185
Jaties, 175
Jobless growth, 50
Joint leadership, 70
Judicial activities, 190, 206
 excesses, 202
Judicial justice, 192
Judicial system, 216
 collapsing of, 37, 58

Kashatriyas, 175
Kashmir, 60, 149
Kothari Commission, 172

Labour-management confrontation, 51
Land reforms, 72
 implementation of, 216, 218
Language riots, 150
Legitimacy, 15
Liberal democratic constitution, 13, 143, 145
 governance, 36
 political system, 17, 24, 30, 43, 46, 48, 51, 60
Liberalisation, 18, 31, 34, 36, 38, 124-125, 126, 129, 138-139, 151, 162, 185
 policy, 101
Life insurance business, 14
Lockouts, 51
Lok Sabha Elections, 23, 67-68, 75, 181, 186
Lucknow district jail, 197

Macro-economic crisis, 31
Madhu Limaye, 200
Mafias, 37, 108
Mahabharata, 25
Mahatma Gandhi, 33, 188
Mahbub-Ul-Haq, 15
Management, modern technology of, 17
Market economy, 36
Market forces, new methodology of, 34

Marketisation, 32
Millitant communalism, 83
Minimum Need Programmes, 105, 118, 130, 136
Misgovernance, 34
Mixed econqmy, system of, 179-180
Modernisation, 18
 capitalist path of, 122
Multi-caste society, 175
Multi-national industrial giants, 32
Multi-party system, 184
Multi-religious society, 83
Multilateral Agreement Investment (MAI), 126
Muslim Women (Protection of Right on Divorce) Bill, 83
Myrdal, Gunnar, 25, 59, 131, 133

Nagarpalikas, 95, 214
Narasimha Rao Government, 22, 76
 new economic policy of, 101
Narayana Rao, G., 201
Narayanan, K. R. (President), 21, 41, 207
National Agenda of the Government (NAG), 124-130,131
 nationalisation of, 125
National Front-Left Front, 67
 combination, 68
National Perspective Plan for Women, 111
National population policy, 134-135
Nehru, Jawahar Lal, 164, 181
Nehru-Gandhi-Rao era, 66
Nehru-Indira Gandhi model, 100
New economic policy, 18, 20, 31, 32, 36, 38, 39, 48, 50, 99, 102-103, 120, 124, 125-126, 138-139, 151, 155, 159, 162
 adoption of, 129
 strategy, 62
New education policy, 55, 157
New forces, impact of, 182-183
New labour policy, 210
New Panchayati Raj system, 20, 92, 98
New social policy, 50
1967 general election, 180-181
1977 general election, 184
1996 Lok Sabha Election, 67-68, 75

Ogg, F A., 64
OMBUDSMAN, 108
Organisational innivation, 106

Pakistan borders, policy of, 56
Palkhiwala, N., 201
Panchayati Raj institutions, 23, 137, 214
 functioning of, 93-94
 recommendations, 94, 96
 system, 117, 119
 women's participation in, 118
Panchayat Samiti, 93
Paranti, Michael, 46
Parliamentary democracy, 65,66, 203
Participatory politics, 183
Participatory socialism, 162
Planning Commission, 119
Plural-federal society, characteristics of, 142-143
 conflict of, 141, 160
 national integration, 158
Pluralist values/provisions, 143, 145
Pokhran nuclear tests, 18
Police functionaries, 61
 intervention, 40, 108
Police forces, democracy in, 154
Politics, caste ideology in, 178, 180
 women participation in, 110, 120
Political community, 15
Political conflicts/violence, 149-150
Political culture, 27-28
 crisis, 22, 24
 development, 164-70, 180, 182
 empowerment, 97
 ingredients of, 168
 governance, 16
Political freedom, 169-170
Political justice, 48-49

Political legitimacy, 24-25
Political opportunities, 182
Political system, 44-45, 89
Political parties, 184
    caste issue by, 178-179
    polarisation of, 73
Political stability, 217
Politico-administrative system, 17, 19, 37-38
Politicisation, 27, 86
Population planning, 134
Population policy, problems/challenges, 135-136
    strategies of, 136, 140
Population stabilisation programmes, 137, 139
Post-election coalition, 69
Poverty, 19, 21, 36, 38, 56, 62, 85, 100, 103, 127, 154-155
    eradication of, 138, 210, 218
Power maximization, 64
Power-sharing, system of, 70
Pre-election alliances, coalition of, 69-70
Private capitalism, 24
Private corporate sector/capitalist development, 13, 16, 19
Privatisation, 18, 21, 31, 34, 36, 38, 101, 120, 124-125, 126, 129, 138-139, 151, 155, 162
Privileges Committee, 197
Public administration, corruption in, 37, 57
Public bureaucracy, 114
Public distribution system, 96, 132
Public investment, 127
Public protests, 59-60
Punjab, 60

Rajiv Gandhi, 72, 187
Reduce subsidies, 132
Religious communities, 142-143, 160
Religious interventions, 81
Reservation facilities, 50
Reservation policy, 21
Romesh Bhandari, 55
Rootless growth, 56
Rural development programmes, 93
Sarkaria Commission, 71
    report, 53
Sarvodaya, 119
Save Hindi agitation, 150
Scheduled Castes and Schedules Tribes, 21, 81, 177
    reservation for, 97
Searchlight, 196
Secessionism/militancy, 58
Secular politicians, 90
Secularisation, 84
Secularism, 17, 26, 50, 60, 66, 78, 90
    concept of, 78-79
    elements of, 159-160
Security problems, 55
Sen, Amartya, 133, 140, 217
Shiman Peres, 70
Singh, V. P., 69, 72
Sixth Five Year Plan, 14
Smugglers, 37
Social challenges, 60
Social justice, 49-50
Social relationships, 46-47
Social security, 132
Social violence, 27
Social welfare programmes, 34, 104
Socio-economic injustice, 84-85
    transformation, 216, 218
Socio-political development, 174, 180
State Election Commission, 92
State-led multiple programmes, 14
Strikes/demonstration, 45, 51, 59
Structural Adjustment Programme (SAP), 32, 53, 101, 115, 129, 138
Syed Mahmood (Justice), 190
Sudras, 175
Supreme Court jurisdiction, 202
Swedeshi philosophy, 126
Switzerland, 71
73rd Constitutional Amendment Act, 23, 92, 96-97, 98, 102, 157

TADA Act, 48, 50
Taxation, 132
Telangana agitation, 150
Terrorism, 25, 37, 58, 60, 131
Terrorist gangs, 149-150
Transformed bureaucracy, 106, 132

Unemployment, 19, 21, 32-33, 38, 57, 60, 85, 100, 103, 116, 120, 122, 127, 131, 138-139, 152, 154-155, 166, 209, 216, 218
  problems of, 58
United Front Coalition Government, 68, 185
United Kingdom, House of Commons of, 195-196
University education, 167, 170-171
  primary function of, 170-171
  responsibilities, 164-165
  scope of, 166-167
Unregulated foreign investment, 126
Untouchability, abolition of, 49
Untouchability (Offence) Act, 82
USSR, 18, 89

Vaishyas, 175
Vajpayee, Atal Behari, 68, 207
Venkatachalaiah, M. N., (Justice), 204
Venkataraman, R., (President), 16, 72-73
Violence, 26

Weberion bureaucracy, 106, 124
Weiner, Myren, 172
Westminster Parliamentary system, 203
Women, coaching centre for, 120
  equal participation, 112
  empowerment, 21
  higher civil services in, 114
  job opportunities, 120
  literacy, 96
  low participation of, 115-116
  participation in politics and decision-making powers, 117, 120
  reservation of seats, 96-97, 116-117
  votes percentage of, 113
Women workers, training programmes for, 119
World Bank, 53, 129, 157
World Trade Organisation (WTO), 126-127, 138-139

Yitzhak Shamir, 71
Yugoslavia, 18, 59

Zamindari System, 70, 129
Zila Parishad, 93